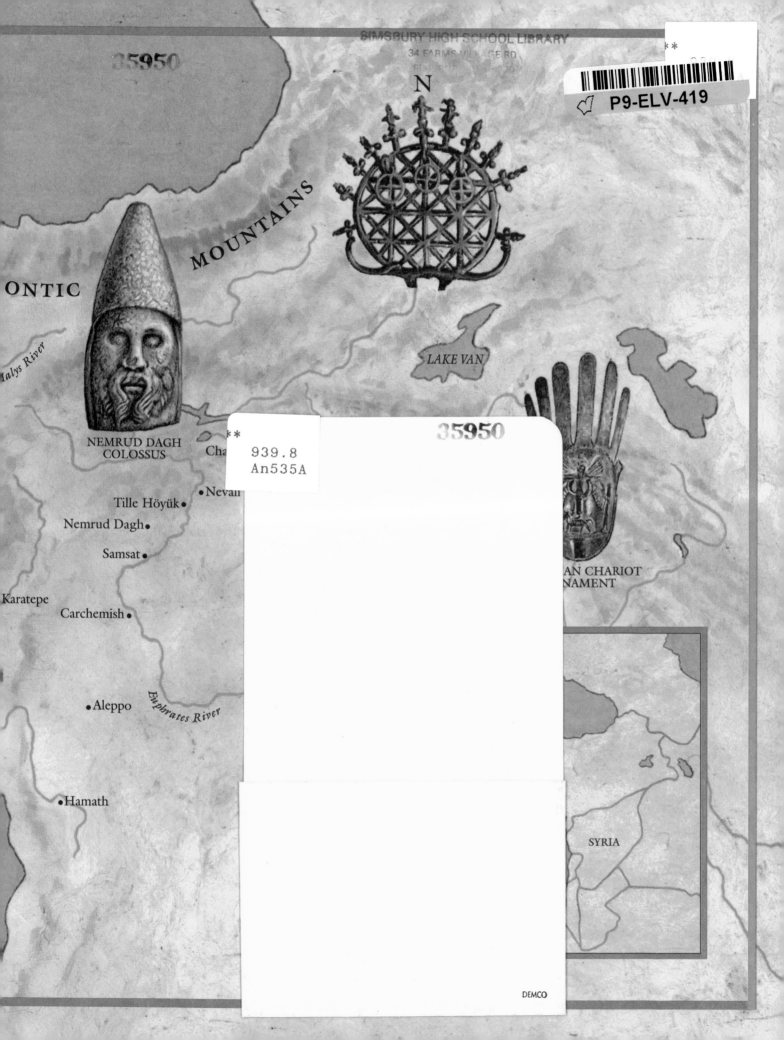

N

PONTIC

MOUNTAINS

Malys River

LAKE VAN

NEMRUD DAGH
COLOSSUS

Cha

Nevai

Tille Höyük

Nemrud Dagh

Samsat

AN CHARIOT
NAMENT

Karatepe

Carchemish

Aleppo

Euphrates River

Hamath

SYRIA

Other Publications:

THE TIME-LIFE COMPLETE
 GARDENER
THE NEW HOME REPAIR AND
 IMPROVEMENT
JOURNEY THROUGH THE MIND
 AND BODY
WEIGHT WATCHERS® SMART CHOICE
 RECIPE COLLECTION
TRUE CRIME
THE AMERICAN INDIANS
THE ART OF WOODWORKING
ECHOES OF GLORY
THE NEW FACE OF WAR
HOW THINGS WORK
WINGS OF WAR
CREATIVE EVERYDAY COOKING
COLLECTOR'S LIBRARY OF THE
 UNKNOWN
CLASSICS OF WORLD WAR II
TIME-LIFE LIBRARY OF CURIOUS AND
 UNUSUAL FACTS
AMERICAN COUNTRY
VOYAGE THROUGH THE UNIVERSE
THE THIRD REICH
MYSTERIES OF THE UNKNOWN
TIME FRAME
FIX IT YOURSELF
FITNESS, HEALTH & NUTRITION
SUCCESSFUL PARENTING
HEALTHY HOME COOKING
UNDERSTANDING COMPUTERS
LIBRARY OF NATIONS
THE ENCHANTED WORLD
THE KODAK LIBRARY OF CREATIVE
 PHOTOGRAPHY
GREAT MEALS IN MINUTES
THE CIVIL WAR
PLANET EARTH
COLLECTOR'S LIBRARY OF THE CIVIL
 WAR
THE EPIC OF FLIGHT
THE GOOD COOK
WORLD WAR II
THE OLD WEST

*For information on and a full description of
any of the Time-Life Books series listed above,
please call 1-800-621-7026 or write:*
Reader Information
Time-Life Customer Service
P.O. Box C-32068
Richmond, Virginia 23261-2068

Cover: Seated with a child on her lap, this golden female wears a disklike headdress that suggests she may be the sun goddess of Arinna, a deity of the Hittite people who dominated Anatolia in the second millennium BC. The mysterious, wide-eyed little figurine is framed by the once equally enigmatic hieroglyphics of a later people known as the Neo-Hittites. The lines of symbols, which were not finally deciphered until 1945, are to be read alternately left to right and then right to left, or "as the ox plows."

End paper: The map, painted by Paul Breeden, indicates the locations of ancient civilizations that flourished in Anatolia, or Asiatic Turkey, from the Neolithic period to the Hellenistic era. Representative artifacts appear near the sites where they were discovered. Breeden also painted the images accompanying the timeline on pages 158-159.

ANATOLIA: CAULDRON OF CULTURES

Time-Life Books is a division of Time Life Inc.

PRESIDENT and CEO: John M. Fahey Jr.

TIME-LIFE BOOKS

MANAGING EDITOR: Roberta Conlan

Director of Design: Michael Hentges
Director of Editorial Operations: Ellen Robling
Director of Photography and Research: John
  Conrad Weiser
Senior Editors: Russell B. Adams Jr., Dale M.
  Brown, Janet Cave, Lee Hassig, Robert
  Somerville, Henry Woodhead
Special Projects Editor: Rita Thievon Mullin
Director of Technology: Eileen Bradley
Library: Louise D. Forstall

PRESIDENT: John D. Hall

Vice President, Director of Marketing:
  Nancy K. Jones
*Vice President, Director of New Product
  Development:* Neil Kagan
Vice President, Book Production: Marjann
  Caldwell
Production Manager: Marlene Zack
Quality Assurance Manager: James King

**Library of Congress
Cataloging in Publication Data**
Anatolia: cauldron of cultures / by the editors
of Time-Life Books.

  p. cm. —(Lost civilizations)
  Includes bibliographical references (p.   )
and index.
  ISBN 0-8094-9108-7
    1. Turkey—Civilization.
    2. Turkey—Antiquities.
  I. Time-Life Books. II. Series.
  DS155.A599 1995
  939'.8—dc20   95-20268
                                            CIP

LOST CIVILIZATIONS

SERIES EDITOR: Dale M. Brown
Administrative Editor: Philip Brandt George

Editorial staff for *Anatolia: Cauldron
  of Cultures*
Art Director: Ellen L. Pattisall
Picture Editor: Charlotte Marine Fullerton
Text Editors: Charles J. Hagner (principal),
  Russell B. Adams Jr., Charlotte Anker
Associate Editors/Research-Writing: Constance
  Contreras, Robin Currie, Jacqueline L.
  Shaffer
Senior Copyeditor: Barbara Fairchild Quarmby
Picture Coordinator: Catherine Parrott
Editorial Assistant: Patricia D. Whiteford
Special Contributors: Anthony Allan, Timothy
  Cooke, Thomas Lewis, Barbara C. Mallen
  (text); Isabel Fucigna, Ann-Louise G. Gates,
  Maureen McHugh, Rita T. Mullin,
  Ellen Riegel, Norma E. Shaw, Elizabeth
  Thompson, Barry N. Wolverton (research);
  Roy Nanovic (index).

Correspondents: Christine Hinze (London),
Christina Lieberman (New York), Maria Vin-
cenza Aloisi (Paris). Valuable assistance was
also provided by: Mehmet Ali Kislali (Ankara);
Elizabeth Kraemer-Singh, Angelica Lemmer
(Bonn); Gay Kavanagh (Brussels); Marlin
Levin (Jerusalem); Judy Aspinall (London);
Elizabeth Brown (New York); Ann Natanson
(Rome); Dick Berry (Tokyo); Traudl Lessing
(Vienna).

The Consultants:

Marie-Henriette Gates is associate professor of
archaeology at Bilkent University in Ankara,
Turkey, and author of *Archaeology in Turkey,*
an annual newsletter published by the *American Journal of Archaeology.* A 25-year veteran
of digs in Italy, Iran, Syria, and Turkey, she has
directed excavations at the ancient port of
Kinet Höyük, classical Issus, since 1992.

Nancy W. Leinwand, administrator of the
American Research Institute in Turkey, spe-
cializes in Near Eastern Art and Archaeology
with a concentration on Anatolia. In addition
to extensive archival research in Turkey, she
has excavated there and in Greece.

Peter Neve, now retired, has been an active
contributor to Hittite archaeology for
more than 40 years. With a doctorate from
Berlin Technical University, he has dug ex-
tensively in Turkey—in and around Hattusha,
near present-day Boghazköy, and at
Karatepe—and in Iraq at Uruk-Warka.

Elizabeth Simpson is a research associate at
The University Museum of the University of
Pennsylvania, where since 1981 she has directed the project to study, draw, conserve, reconstruct, and publish the collection of wooden
furniture excavated at the site of Gordion,
Turkey. She also teaches ancient art and archaeology at the Bard Graduate Center for
Studies in the Decorative Arts in New York.

Robert Lindley Vann is professor of architecture at the University of Maryland and director of that university's archaeological survey of
ancient harbors in Turkey. Concentrating on
building materials and techniques of construction in the ancient world as well as on maritime history and underwater archaeology, he
has extensive field experience in Turkey and in
most of the rest of the Mediterranean world.

Special Contributor:

Helga Kohl, who provided the outline and
much of the research for this book, has been a
longtime student of Turkey and a frequent
visitor to that country. A former *Time* re-
searcher and reporter and Time-Life Books
staff member, she has also been a European
stringer for *Time, Life, Fortune,* and Time-Life
Books. As a major contributor to *Lost Civilizations,* she did the initial development work
on *Egypt: Land of the Pharaohs, Ramses II:
Magnificence on the Nile,* and *Wondrous
Realms of the Aegean.*

This volume is one in a series that explores
the worlds of the past, using the finds of archaeologists and other scientists to bring ancient peoples and their cultures vividly to life.

ANATOLIA: CAULDRON OF CULTURES

By the Editors of Time-Life Books

TIME-LIFE BOOKS, ALEXANDRIA, VIRGINIA

CONTENTS

ANCIENT TURKEY: LAND OF FORGOTTEN KINGDOMS

Rich in ruins of its Roman, Greek, and earlier cultures, Turkey attracted 19th-century explorers and artists. This 1841 sketch of a pillar tomb is by George Scharf, who traveled with British archaeologist Sir Charles Fellows and went on to become the first head of London's National Portrait Gallery.

When French archaeologist and explorer Charles-Félix-Marie Texier set out across Turkey's central Anatolian highlands in 1834, he had a goal: to find the ruins of a Roman settlement called Tavium. But his quest could not be characterized as determined; Texier went from village to village, asking if there were any ruins nearby. Often, of course, the answer was yes, as it was at Boghazköy, today known as Boghazkäle, a village in a sparsely populated area 90 miles east of the modern Turkish capital of Ankara. Following some of the locals, who said they would take him to a site nearby, he made a long climb into the craggy hills above the town, where he beheld the ruins of a fortified wall that had boasted guard towers and a pair of gates, one flanked by great statues of stone lions, the other bearing a larger-than-life kinglike figure. Within the wall was an area of at least one square mile; there Texier came across huge blocks of stone, obviously the remnants of enormous foundations.

An eager villager then led Texier on an hour-long hike along a twisting path to what seemed to be yet more of the towering limestone outcroppings so characteristic of the area. But as the Frenchman drew nearer the rocks, he began to see just why his guide had been so keen to show him the site. Along two apparently natural galleries strode a stately procession of 66 sculptured figures, some carrying great curved swords and wearing conical crowns, others in

flowing robes. And on closer inspection, he also made out a wealth of hieroglyphs the like of which he had never seen. To the locals, the place was known as Yazilikaya, or "Inscribed rock."

Trying to make sense of the figures carved into the rock, Texier guessed that they were a mixture of Paphlagonians, an ancient people from the Black Sea region, and mythological Amazons. And as for the great walled-in settlement rising above Boghazköy, Texier was equally uncertain: "The grandeur and the peculiar nature of the ruins," he wrote later, "perplexed me extraordinarily when I attempted to give the city its historical name." Convinced that they were not of Roman origin, he speculated that they marked the site of Pteria, a town seized from Persia's Cyrus the Great in the sixth century BC by Croesus, the ruler of a kingdom called Lydia. What Texier had in fact stumbled upon in this desolate spot were the ruins of Hattusha, capital of the ancient kingdom of the Hittites, a great people who, amazingly, had been lost to history for over 2,000 years.

Texier was one of a growing number of globe-trotting Europeans who journeyed through the lands of the Middle East during the 19th century. Dubbed the "wandering scholars," these men were intellectual adventurers, catholic in their inquiries, delving into the geography, geology, archaeology, and botany of what they supposed to be the sweep of human history. Often enduring great privations,

This is how the ruins of the Hittite capital of Hattusha looked to French explorer Charles Texier when he stumbled upon them in 1834. Despite being unaware of what he had found, Texier took copious notes and made detailed sketches of the entire area. His drawings and records would prove crucial to later scholars as they tried to make sense of the artifacts that would lead to the rediscovery of the Hittite empire.

they doggedly went about the business of filling in the empty spaces on imperial maps and hauling artifacts back to Western museums.

The problem and the passion of early travelers in Anatolia, or Asiatic Turkey, which makes up 97 percent of modern Turkey (the remaining 3 percent is located on the European side of the Bosporus), was to match the rubble they saw strewn across the landscape with the descriptions of cities, temples, and palaces found in their Bibles and classical texts. Centuries of earthquakes, floods, and erosion—not to mention wars—had shattered, stirred, and covered much of the detritus of millennia. Especially after the Seleucids—among the three eventual inheritors of Alexander the Great's empire—and the Romans clear-cut many of Anatolia's forests and gouged out countless mines, erosion ate away the thin topsoil of the region's highlands, choking rivers and inundating lowland sites of early habitation with tons of water-borne silt. The ruins not buried or thrown down by storm, earthquake, or marauders were chipped away by frost, wind, and rain as if by a determined trio of destructive masons.

A place of staggering diversity—geographic as well as ethnic and historic—Anatolia defies easy classification. Measuring about 400 miles from north to south, it extends over 1,000 miles east to west, for half of this distance seeming to thrust out from the Asian continent toward Greece (to the Romans, in fact, the land was known as

Following in Texier's footsteps, Sir William Hamilton made this drawing of the rock shrine Yazilikaya near Hattusha around 1840. Like Texier, the archaeologist was pursuing classical Roman ruins and was unaware that he was standing face-to-face with a pantheon of Hittite gods and goddesses. Texier believed the figures to be Amazons; Hamilton thought the scene commemorated a treaty between the Persians and Lydians.

Asia Minor). A Turkish poet provides an apt image: "This country shaped like the head of a mare, / Coming full gallop from far-off Asia, / To stretch into the Mediterranean."

Anatolia is bounded by three seas: the Mediterranean to the south, the Aegean to the west, and the Black to the north. Archaeologist Seton Lloyd, viewing it from the east, likes to see it as an upright "open left hand, the thumb curled inward to represent the Taurus Mountains," which run along the Mediterranean, and the Anti-Taurus, which fortify the borders with Iraq and Syria to the south. "The palm would then suggest the hollow plateau," the arid interior with its central salt lake; "the heel of the hand the eastern massif," which defines the boundaries with Georgia, Armenia, and Iran; and the splayed fingers "the diminishing ranges that extend westward to find their echo in the islands of the Aegean."

Through the ages such topographical diversity imposed corresponding differences in human behavior and settlement patterns. The effect of these natural niches, over time, was to give rise to a patchwork of differing cultures, each adapted to its particular locality, those of the rugged interior being quite distinct from those of the mountains or the more salubrious coastal region. Over these mountains, plains, and valleys successive waves of peoples from Asia and the Middle East met, traded, and fought. They were succeeded by Greeks and Romans, lured by the country's riches and its location as an entry point to Asia. In time, Anatolia became the heart of the Ottoman Empire, founded by Turkic tribes from Central Asia; Ottoman territory once extended from Austria through the Balkans across the Middle East to the Persian Gulf and into North Africa.

Anatolia's wandering scholars were, of course, aware of the region's reputation as a bridge between east and west. "There is scarcely a spot of ground however small that does not contain some relic of antiquity," declared the Royal Geological Society's William Hamilton after returning from one of his journeys there in 1842 . But the scholars, through no shortcomings of their own, were viewing it through the limited lenses of their day. To Hamilton and his colleagues, this was a land of Greek scholars, Persian kings, Macedonian conquerors, Roman emperors, and Byzantine bishops; they had no inkling of the others who had preceded these ancients, the Hittites among them. Filled with a romantic vision of the past, they saw Anatolia as birthplace of such major figures as the poet Homer, the avaricious King Midas, Herodotus, the "Father of History," and Paul the Apostle. It was here after his defeat of Pharnaces, ruler of the Black Sea kingdom of Pontus, that Julius Caesar proclaimed the celebrated words, "*Veni, vidi, vici*—I came, I saw, I conquered."

While the scholars rightly saw Anatolia as an ancient land, with more Greek monuments than Greece, more Roman settlements than Italy, they blithely attributed its layers of history to outsiders. Of Anatolia's contributions, Hamilton was derisive. "Asia Minor was only of secondary importance when the dynasties of the Pharaohs ruled in Egypt," he said. "When the sons of Israel went down to buy corn [grain] of the Egyptian kings, we read not of the civilization of Asia Minor, nor did she produce at any period such structures as the Pyramids, or the Temples of the Nile, to record the talents of her architects, or the perseverance of her people." Anatolia's importance, it seemed, stemmed from its location, and the land had served as a battleground long enough to hold a rich litter of other people's history. Under the litter lay the lost civilizations of Anatolia.

Jealously guarded by the Ottoman Turks—who restricted outsiders' access to the country—Anatolia held tight its secrets. Those early explorers who were allowed to poke about in its dead cities and along its deserted Roman highways were, quite literally, scratching the surface. Only in the next century, when the new Turkish republic ended the official paranoia of the Ottoman Empire and introduced the discipline of archaeology into the country's university system, did researchers armed with modern technology and attitudes begin to ask new questions about the ruins of Anatolia—and get surprising answers. Not just a caravan route between more interesting destinations—"a bridge with lofty parapets," as the English antiquarian Sir William Ramsay put it—Anatolia was shown to be an important hub of early development, advanced in metallurgy and farming methods, a cradle of civilization to rival in its accomplishments its more illustrious neighbors in Mesopotamia and Egypt.

The eventual decipherment of clay tablets and stone inscriptions would reveal that Anatolia had been a land awash in cultural tidal waves for longer than anyone had dreamed. By the 16th century BC it was dominated by the Hittites, an Indo-European people, whose entire legacy had been reduced to a few enigmatic mentions in the Bible until their rediscovery in the 20th century. Then, the evidence of their own archives of clay-tablet records, along with those of the Egyptian pharaohs with whom they had a long and turbulent relationship, showed that the Hittites had been prominent until their empire was swept away by some great regional upheaval at the end of the 13th century BC.

For 500 years thereafter, while Ionian, Dorian, and Aeolian Greeks—collectively known as the eastern Greeks—made the short trip across the Aegean to colonize the coastal areas of Anatolia, the interior of the country was a cultural kaleidoscope. Much of it was dominated for several hundred years by a federation of tribal peoples from the Balkans called the Phrygians, whose King Midas took a place in the legends of the world for the opulence of his capital at Gordion. Meanwhile, city-state vestiges of the old Hittite empire persisted beyond the Taurus Mountains of the south. In the farthest eastern reaches of Anatolia, a remarkable highland kingdom called Urartu flourished for three centuries, then, as in the case of the Hittites, was utterly forgotten until the mid-20th century. And in the west, between the Phrygians and the band of Greek coastal settlements, the Lydians not only retained their independence but grew in influence. In the sixth century BC, after invasions by Cimmerian nomads from the Caucasus had weakened the Phrygians, the Lydians under King Croesus extended their power onto the central Anatolian plains and even dominated some of the Greek city-states.

Waves of invaders continued to engulf Anatolia, however, first from one direction, then another. In 547 BC, the Persian king Cyrus the Great, on his way to building an empire that would reach from Egypt to northwestern India, smashed the Lydian capital of Sardis in western Anatolia and divided the land into satrapies, or governorships. Chafing under Persian rule, the eastern Greeks finally revolted in 499 BC, with the help of Athens on the Greek mainland. Cyrus's successor, Darius, put down the uprising, but it took him five years to do so, and afterward he launched a series of vengeful attacks on Greece itself that would be remembered as the Persian Wars.

Later, in 334 BC, Macedonia's Alexander the Great crossed from Europe into Anatolia to liberate the Greeks there and challenge Persia. Near the Granicus River in northwestern Anatolia, Alexander met and soundly defeated an enemy army under Darius III that was three times the size of his own. Next, he marched down the Aegean coast and then across to Issos along the eastern Mediterranean, where he again routed the Persians. By the time of Alexander's untimely death in Babylon in 323 BC, his all-conquering armies had

The somber face on this marble bust belongs to Herodotus, the "Father of History." Although he lived for a time in Athens and is best known for his accounts of the Greek wars with Persia, Herodotus was an Anatolian, born in the coastal city of Halicarnassus. He begins his most famous work, the Histories, *in Lydia with the ascent of Croesus, one of the most famous of Anatolian kings.*

pushed his empire as far east as the Indus Valley. The empire was divided among Alexander's generals; one of them, Seleucus, received Babylonia, giving rise to the Seleucid dynasty, which would take over Anatolia and dominate it for 250 years.

In the second century BC the Romans began to arrive in Anatolia, and with them came a peace and a stability under which the region would thrive. Eventually Constantinople, today known as Istanbul, became the center of the Roman Empire and, later, the capital of the Eastern Roman or Byzantine Empire. In the accounts of this grand sweep of human events—the epic poems, legends, songs, and stories—the people of Anatolia were for the most part invisible, presumed to have been little more than onlookers at an intersection of history. Slowly at first, then with a series of stunning revelations, they have emerged to take their proper place.

The gentleman travelers who trekked across Anatolia in the 1800s were, like the intrepid Texier, on the lookout for sites that had been important in the classical age. A few years after Texier's discoveries at Boghazköy in 1834, Sir Charles Fellows began to explore the country he regarded as "a part of Greece." Excited by the monuments that he saw but frustrated by a lack of maps or published accounts on the classical legacy of Anatolia, he determined to make a survey. After a return trip in 1840, he wrote with pride that he had "discovered the remains of 11 cities not denoted on any map." Although he was more interested in the location than the contents of the ruins, Sir Charles's description of one of his finds, the fifth-century-BC city of Pinara near the Mediterranean coast in the southwest, was intriguing. There he beheld the ancient Greek theater "in a very perfect state," along with the remains of massive buildings and tombs that one might have expected of an Ionian city. But from its center, he wrote, "rises a singular round rocky cliff, literally speckled all over with tombs. There must be some thousands, and most of them are merely oblong holes cut in the perpendicular front of the rock, which is apparently inaccessible." Having sketched the marvel, and inked it on his map, Sir Charles moved on. When his work was done, he reckoned, he had identified "24 of the 36 cities mentioned by Pliny [the Elder] as having left remains still seen in his age," the mid-first century AD. And, he added, "I also observed many other piles of ruins."

When railway engineer John Turtle Wood left England for Ephesus, near Anatolia's Aegean coast, he too was searching for the classical—for remnants of the Great Temple of Diana *(pages 122-123)*, judged by the ancients to be the most beautiful of the Seven Wonders of the World. But unlike the sites seen by Fellows, this monument to the goddess, called Artemis by the Greeks, preserved no traces above ground. Measuring 425 by 255 feet, the ruins of the temple and its 127 fluted columns—each had soared 60 feet—had been buried under a covering of alluvial soil brought by floodwaters of the nearby Cayster River. Recent accounts of the site provided little help. One visitor to Ephesus during the 18th century had recorded, "We now seek in vain for the temple; the city is prostrate: and the goddess gone." So, with only the writings of classical authors to guide him, Wood began work in the spring of 1863, sinking the first of hundreds of trial holes across the countryside in an attempt to locate the temple Pliny had described as the *Graecae magnificae*.

In his quest for the elusive temple, Wood had to contend with a host of difficulties. Inexplicable halts to the dig were called by the pashas of the nearby port city of Smyrna, who, wrote Wood, "succeeded one another so rapidly that as soon as I had propitiated one of them I found myself obliged to conciliate another." At least one of these high Ottoman officials was not without a sense of humor, however. Since all duplicates of antiquities found at Ephesus had to be left for the Turks themselves, he asked Wood to inform him when the excavations turned up "the Temple of Diana in duplicate."

Labor proved another headache, and Wood was always looking for good workers. Although he eventually employed over 300 men, he was constantly beset with holdups and delays. The fever that was generated by the area's river marshes could account for as many as a quarter of his workers being out at any one time, and toiling 14 to 15 hours a day himself, Wood became a frequent victim of ill health. Work was impossible during the hot season, which began in May and lasted until autumn, and during the more temperate months downpours often swamped the excavations. Digging would halt long before the pits were flooded with water, however; "ever so

A RACE AGAINST RISING WATERS

Across southeastern Turkey a network of dams and irrigation canals is being built along the Tigris and Euphrates Rivers as part of a government plan to transform the arid region into an agricultural Eden.

Remote and in many places inaccessible, southeastern Anatolia was unknown to most archaeologists before the dam projects began. But starting in 1975 archaeological surveys have discovered hundreds of important sites that are threatened by the dams. In an effort to rescue as many of these as possible, the Turkish Department of Antiquities invited archaeologists to participate in an international rescue operation. Americans, Germans, French, Dutch, and Turks responded. One archaeologist ruefully remarked that "the dams are a great boon to our understanding of the cultural development

of the region, wonderful and terrible at the same time."

In the race to excavate threatened sites, shortcuts have to be taken. At the 14-century-BC site of Tille Höyük *(seen above before and during flooding from the Ataturk Dam in 1990)* the scale of the excavation was reduced several times during the British Institute of Archaeology's 12 years of work. Methods have also been adapted to fit the fast pace; picks and shovels often replace the more traditional trowel. At Samsat *(below)* workers were assigned

the unusual task of demolishing Roman walls; underneath lay Hittite, Urukian, and Bronze Age remains.

Professor Nimet Özgüc, director of the Samsat project and one of Turkey's leading archaeologists, remarked that "it would take at least 100 years to understand this place." But her team had only 11 members, and 1989 was the last season before the rising Euphrates River closed in. The rescue of other sites continues, however, and more is revealed about Anatolia's buried past.

Nineteenth-century explorers did not always have to rough it, as this sketch by George Scharf demonstrates. Carefully labeled, it shows his and Sir Charles Fellows's accommodations in Anatolia—a wood frame house with a thick floor matting, beds, linens, china, a small library, and even a fruit-bearing orange branch, hanging from a rafter. The house also had a fireplace. Fellows is seated and facing the reader; Scharf is on the near side; and the man standing is an architect who bunked with them.

little rain was sufficient to stop the works," the incredulous and rain-accustomed Englishman lamented, for "the Turks do not work in the rain."

The 30-day fast of Ramadan and the feast that followed also caused delays, "the men being too weak for work during the fast, and absent from the works during the feast." Unpredictable halts also had to be dealt with—including the workers' reaction to a sudden eclipse of the moon. "The Turks do not understand eclipses," wrote Wood, "and, on the occurrence of such phenomena, still think that some monster is endeavoring to devour the sun or moon. This evening they beat their drums and fired off guns to warn off the monster, and in doing so they shot a cow by accident, which they feasted on the next day."

Besides hiring Turks, who made up the majority of his work force, Wood recruited a large number of Greeks and at one time had nearly 100 Arabs in his employ. "They were exceedingly quarrelsome," he wrote of the Arabs, and since they were constantly trying to outdo the other diggers—"invariably the first in finishing their work"—there was "a great danger of their coming to blows with the Turks." An even greater risk existed of the Turks getting into fights with the Greeks. Wood found the latter were "generally quick and intelligent," although, he recalled, "their numerous holidays, all of which they kept most religiously by sitting at cafes dressed up in their best clothes, made them very undesirable workmen."

While Wood managed to head off most trouble at the work site, he remembered a fracas that broke out at a nearby village on a Sunday evening: "One of the Turkish workmen, having taken too much raki [an anise-flavored liquor], was singing in a maudlin way and making a fool of himself as he passed a priest and some other Greeks who were seated outside a cafe. . . . One of the Greeks very foolishly ridiculed the Turk, who, not too drunk to see and to resent the insult, stopped and cursed the Greeks and their religion. The priest upon this exclaimed, 'Why do you curse my children?' The Turk replied by striking the priest with his stick. All the Greeks, chiefly agricultural laborers, then rose up and began to assault the Turk, who laid about him furiously with his stick, and was soon joined by some of his fellow workmen." The fight became a pitched battle involving about 60 men armed with sticks and stones, the Turks finally routing the Greeks. About 20 men were badly wounded, among the worst of them the Greek priest—"bruised from head to foot." Complained Wood, "I lost the services of some of my best men by this affair."

Despite all the difficulties, the team of diggers was closing in on the temple. On the last day of 1869, its marble pavement was at last found at a depth of nearly 20 feet below the surface. By this time, even the locals were intrigued to know just what had been discovered. One day the site was visited by the district's *mudir*, or deputy tax collector. "I told him," recalled Wood, "they were the remains of an ancient mosque or church, in the time of the Greeks, when they did not worship the one true God, but had many gods, male and fe-

Brought along to record the landscape just as Fellows found it, Scharf frequently depicted earthquake-ravaged sites, such as the toppled Chimera Tomb above. In this case, though, natural disaster proved to be good fortune, since half the tomb's lid lay buried, protected by the earth. The well-preserved motif of four Persian horses pulling a chariot and trampling a chimera is shown by Scharf in his detailed watercolor (inset).

17

ducers. Only then can some people take the time to study and practice the craft of the metalsmith and the jeweler, and the attendant social distinctions increase the demand for personal ornaments.

These conditions, as further diggings would show, had long been in place in Anatolia. And as metalworkers became more proficient, they experimented, finding that some ores containing more than one metal were better for casting than others. In time, the smiths of Alaca Höyük began to form their own alloys by deliberately mixing metals for appearance. Eventually, metalworkers throughout the Middle East began to heat a blend of tin and copper to very high temperatures to produce a very useful alloy called bronze.

Harder than copper and easier to cast, bronze also kept an edge longer and could be sharpened more easily. From about 3000 BC to 1000 BC, when iron replaced it, bronze was associated with vigorous economic and social advancements such as the rise of the great cities of Sumer and the later empires of Mesopotamia. To meet the demand for bronze weapons and utensils, the manufacture of the metal had to progress beyond the level of community craft to that of a regional industry. But as archaeologists began pushing into more and more of the cultural provinces of Anatolia, they failed to find there—or indeed anywhere else in the Middle East—a single major source of tin or a single large furnace used for smelting tin ore. Anatolia was rich in copper deposits, and excavations at places such as Alaca Höyük revealed evidence of furnaces that had been used to smelt copper, but not tin. Toward the end of the 20th century, the mystery persisted.

Once again Anatolia provided one possible answer to this epochal puzzle. In a press conference in January 1994, Aslihan Yener of the University of Chicago's Oriental Institute announced the results of her excavations at an ancient village called Göltepe, in the Taurus Mountains 60 miles north of the southern Anatolian town of Tarsus. The place had been occupied, she said, from around 3290 BC to about 1840 BC by between

SEEING DOUBLE IN ANATOLIA

The ancient Anatolians showed a curious predilection for creatures with two heads, as evidenced by some of their sculptures. They used twin images as far back as Neolithic times, and created its most durable form in double eagles like the one below, found among Hittite ruins. Double eagles have flown on the flags of the Byzantine and Holy Roman Empires, czarist Russia, and Austria-Hungary, and in the 1990s became the national symbol of the new Russia. In all cases the bird looks both ways, perhaps signifying all-seeing power or, as in the case of Russia, looking both at the nation's past and toward its future.

This rotund idol from Kanesh, near the modern town of Kayseri, dramatizes the basic geometry of twin-headed sculpture: the two heads coming together into oneness, which is represented by a sphere. Made of marble, it dates from the third millennium BC.

This goddess from the Neolithic site of Chatal Höyük was carved from black stone around the sixth millennium BC. One head is larger than the other, leading some to conclude that the two heads represent mother and daughter.

The handle on the back of this 14th-century-BC clay duck indicates it was a vessel of some sort. Found at the site of the imperial Hittite capital of Hattusha, it is an example of the decorated ritual animal rhytons seen carried by attendants to the gods in Hittite rock reliefs.

500 and 1,000 people. Their livelihood was derived from a nearby tin mine. Yener's team had found a network of tunnels, extending more than a mile into the mountain, that contained residues of low-grade tin ore. The narrowness of the tunnels—just two feet across—suggested that children had done the brutally hard work of excavating the ore, a suspicion that was borne out by the discovery in the mine of several skeletons of youngsters between 12 and 15 years old.

But the villagers of Göltepe had been involved in far more than grubbing ore from the interior of a mountain. In the village, Yener and her colleagues found the remains of tens of thousands of small ceramic crucibles—the largest the size of a cooking pot—that provided an important clue to the central mystery of the Bronze Age. Analysis with x-rays and electron microscopes revealed traces of slag—residue from metal smelting—that held as much as 30 percent tin. Yener eventually worked out how the smelting had been done.

It seems that the miners first built fires at the mine face to heat and soften the ore so they could more readily chisel it out with stone tools. After hauling it to the surface, they ground the ore to a coarse powder, washed it, and panned for any sizable nuggets of tin. The remaining powder they spread in the small crucibles with alternating layers of charcoal, which was set alight. Experiments showed that they may have blown on the fire through reed pipes, raising the temperature to a surprisingly high 2,000°F. At this point the tin content

24

would melt and separate from the ore to leave droplets of tin encased in slag. Crushing the slag would reveal the pure tin.

The skills of these tin smelters from Göltepe was evidence that Early Bronze Age Anatolia was more than an area of farmers. The inhabitants of this remote valley showed that the region participated fully in the technological knowledge of the contemporary Middle East. In 1938, other advanced communities were found to have existed elsewhere in Anatolia at an even earlier date. The discovery came from a mound 400 miles south of Alaca Höyük, at the edge of the town of Mersin on the Mediterranean coast. This time, British researchers found themselves digging their way not only into the Early Bronze Age but also through it and into the preceding Chalcolithic period, the transition from the Stone Age to the Bronze Age.

At the level of about 4500 BC, the archaeologists chanced on evidence of an unusual event. At that time the village—which, it was later learned, had been occupied even in the Stone Age—had been leveled and then systematically rebuilt. The new settlement was enclosed by a massive wall with towers overlooking its gate and with narrow windows through which defenders could sling stones and not be exposed to return fire. There were standard quarters for members of a garrison—a living room next to a courtyard where piles of stones for ammunition were kept. Finer quarters were provided for persons of higher rank. Such features, familiar as they were to students of later ages, revealed to the British team another milestone for Anatolia: Mersin ranks as one of the earliest known military fortresses in the world.

Fascinating as were the finds at Mersin and Alaca Höyük, Anatolia was about to yield more about its prehistoric past. As modern archaeology began to hit its stride in Turkey in the 1940s and 1950s, it turned up abundant proof of still earlier human habitation. In 1947, Turkish archaeologist Kilic Kökten found the first evidence of Neanderthals in Anatolia, at 12,000-year-old

Thought to represent the god of the hunt, this bronze stag with inlaid silver detail was among many similar stags discovered in the royal graves at Alaca Höyük. Employing the lost-wax process, the artist skillfully used the runnels through which the molten metal had been poured as a mount for the animal.

Karain Cave, in the Taurus Mountains 20 miles northwest of the Mediterranean town of Antalya. And four years later, British archaeologist James Mellaart began searching southern Anatolia for the origins of the people who had migrated around 1200 BC to Palestine to become known as the Philistines. "Instead," he wrote later, "I found hundreds of sites which were very much earlier than that—and much earlier than archaeologists in those days thought possible." One of them was a substantial mound near the town of Konya, on the southern edge of the central Anatolian plateau. The Englishman may have been encouraged by a local tradition that claimed Konya had been the first town to surface after the Noachian Flood.

Mellaart first saw the mound on a bright November morning in 1952. He had been collecting sherds from likely-looking sites since April, traveling mostly on foot, carefully husbanding a slim stipend of £250. Suffering from dysentery and with winter coming, he recalled that he felt "depressed at the sight of how much there was left to do—there seemed to be prehistoric mounds stretching all around me as far as the horizon." But this one, on the dusty Konya Plain, was special. It rose gently to a height of 58 feet, covered an area of 32 acres, and wrote Mellaart, "even from nine kilometres away it looked distinctly inviting." But winter was too close for him to investigate the mound that year, and other commitments intervened the next. In fact, it would be nine years before the intrepid archaeologist could start excavating the mound at Konya called Chatal Höyük. Meanwhile, he began exploring a site near the village of Hacilar, 135 miles to the west, where strata led him back to 6300 BC, in the Neolithic period when humans, who had previously relied on hunting and gathering, first began to cultivate crops, domesticate animals, and develop communities. But he also found evidence of a much earlier settlement that dated to about 7500 BC. "This made the site as old as anything known in Mesopotamia," he declared, "and vindicated my belief that Anatolia was no cultural backwater."

Mellaart was intrigued by the fact that a span of a full millennium separated the abandonment of the oldest village at Hacilar and the building of the later settlement. He felt sure that among the mounds of the Anatolian plateau there was a site that could, as he put it, "fill in this hiatus of a thousand years." In 1958 he and two friends took another, casual look at Chatal Höyük.

On inspecting the western side of the mound, Mellaart noted that the prevailing winds had scoured the surface of its covering

Considered one of the most exquisite stylized statuettes of Early Bronze Age Anatolia, this goddess is made of silver, with a gold-plated head, ankle bracelets, and breast bands. Just nine inches tall, the idol is thought to represent fertility.

of "turf and ruinweed," like a bold hand lifting a veil on a hidden past. Mellaart stared in awe at what had been revealed. "I could see traces of burnt walls, forming a rectangular pattern," he recalled. "It could mean only one thing—there were many houses. There was no doubt in my mind that these lower levels were Neolithic. And when my friends reported that they had found Neolithic remains at the top as well, I realized that Chatal Höyük was all one huge Neolithic city."

After wrapping up work at Hacilar on May 17, 1961, Mellaart and his team began the formal excavation of a one-acre section of the mound on the Konya Plain. "Ten days later," he reported, "the first Neolithic paintings ever found on man-made walls were exposed, and it was clear that Chatal Höyük was no ordinary site." In uncovering what eventually turned out to be 14 levels of habitation at the mound, the archaeologists might have expected to find evidence of a small, primitive village showing signs of experimentation with the first vestiges of agriculture and community. Instead, they unearthed a Stone Age settlement of extraordinary size and development.

The city consisted of more than 1,000 small, rectangular houses made of sun-dried mud brick, huddled together in the manner of a honeycomb much like the Native American pueblo dwellings of Arizona and New Mexico. The house walls facing outward on the edge of the settlement were built without openings to form a solid outer perimeter, probably for security reasons. But even the interior walls had no openings on the ground level, for the city was virtually streetless and access was by ladder from the flat roofs. Ladders also connected one roof to another to form the city's communal areas.

Inside, the rooms were cramped, some just 10 by 13 feet. Supporting pillars, made of mud brick or wood timbers, were covered with plaster and painted red. Plastered platforms provided beds, tables, and the like, and many of the walls were decorated with murals. They are among the oldest known wall paintings in the world, and the best preserved. No other site has provided as much artwork. The images at Chatal Höyük consist of animals, handprints, and geometric patterns, as well as naturalistic still-life scenes, lifelike depictions of people dancing and hunting, and the world's first landscape, a view of the town against a backdrop of a nearby erupting volcano.

Many of Chatal Höyük's structures were not just residences. Some may have been shrines containing vestiges of what must have been a fertility cult—stone and clay figurines and paintings and reliefs of a mother goddess (*page 29*). Artistic endeavor was evident in

27

many of the other finds. Pottery, flints, beads, obsidian implements, and ornaments made from copper and lead were all of a high quality. The city's inhabitants also made use of textiles: Found in graves beneath the floors of houses were remnants of cloth made from linen that are among the earliest known textiles, as well as equipment for spinning and weaving. The townsfolk benefited not only from well-established agriculture—there was evidence of grain cultivation and of domesticated sheep—but from far-flung trade as well, involving the exchange of obsidian used in tool and weapon production for ornamental seashells from the distant Mediterranean shore.

In its economic and cultural achievements, Chatal Höyük was not alone, however. It was among many contemporary developed sites in the Middle East. But as one of the largest Neolithic settlements in the world—remarkable in its level of preservation—the city represents a pinnacle of progress in Anatolia. At a time when agriculture was just beginning in the Balkans and Europeans still relied on hunting for food, Chatal Höyük stands as a triumph of a new age.

Meanwhile, further excavation in Karain Cave and discoveries of other Paleolithic sites continued to extend Anatolia's human chronology into the past—to 10,000 BC at Karain and at a subsequently found companion cave called Öküzini, and to perhaps 125,000 BC in the caves of Yarimburgaz, near Istanbul, which yielded 960 flaked-stone tools. And the early advent of the Neolithic revolution in Anatolia was confirmed by later digs at the central Anatolian site of Ashikli Höyük, a Neolithic city even older than Chatal Höyük with similarly complex architecture although without the wall paintings *(pages 32-33)*.

Thus, for tens of thousands of years, dramatic cultural change has been a constant for the residents of Anatolia. While the picture of the region's prehistory is still far from complete, the archaeological revelations of the 20th century have made clear that at every upward step taken by the human species—from hunter-gatherer to farmer, from stone tools to metal, from cave to city—the people of Anatolia were in the vanguard. Moreover, seen in the light of the recent discoveries, the emergence of Anatolia's first great empire, that of the Hittites, can no longer be ascribed solely to the arrival in the land of the Indo-Europeans but must be seen as the outcome of countless centuries of growth in diversity and character achieved against great odds in Anatolia's for- bidding but fertile central plateau.

MILESTONES OF CIVILIZATION

As a crossroads of cultures, Turkey is rich with relics of the past. But when archaeology got under way there in the 19th century no one could have dreamed just how multilayered a repository of history it would prove to be. Especially productive are the central plateau and the southeastern region through which the Tigris and Euphrates Rivers flow—areas examined in this essay. There, sites go back to the Neolithic period, some 10,000 years ago, when people began shifting from their age-old hunter-gatherer way of life to the more settled one of farming, founding villages in the process.

Some of humankind's first steps toward civilization were thus taken in Anatolia, more than 6,000 years before the rise of Sumer. Indeed, one of the oldest known cities in the world is Chatal Höyük, a farming and trading center that flourished between 6000 and 5600 BC and gave rise to many outstanding achievements. Remarkably, during its long existence, it seems never

to have been attacked. Is this a sign that Neolithic peoples were more peaceable than their descendants would eventually be?

The full-bodied figure above, considered to be at least 8,000 years old, is one of the earliest representations of a female. The eight-inch-high, baked-clay statue turned up, appropriately enough, in the grain bin of a Chatal Höyük shrine, for the subject is believed to be the mother goddess, the embodiment of fertility and fecundity. It was in her, apparently, that farmers put their trust as they evolved their new ways of living, learning not only to plant crops and raise animals but also to weave cloth, use metal, and in time, to make fired pottery. Portrayed here as well fed, she is giving birth, guarded by two—real or symbolic—leopards. Interestingly, female deities were to dominate the central Anatolian pantheon for thousands of years before male gods gained the upper hand; it might be said that women led the way to civilization.

Nevali Cori
ENTRY TO A TIME MACHINE

Nevali Cori is one of the oldest permanent settlements ever excavated. The site dates back 10,000 years. Digging here was conducted in the 1980s and 1990s by a German-Turkish team. The group's leader, Harald Hauptmann, saw the project as providing "direct entry to a time machine." Among the discoveries were 27 houses devoted primarily to food storage, as revealed by the presence of grain and the bones of gazelles and other wild animals; but the most exciting find was the temple shown below.

Here—in a room that measured 45 by 45 feet and was laid, surprisingly enough, with a terrazzo floor—several limestone figures were uncovered. And a cult statue may once have occupied a niche. Hauptmann thinks Nevali Cori's religion-minded inhabitants were first drawn to the area and also motivated to settle down by the abundance of game. Hauptmann also believes hunter-gatherers elsewhere may have been similarly prompted, beginning to farm the surrounding areas only much later.

At the center of Nevali Cori's stone-walled temple a pillar still stands. Displaying what appear to be two arms and hands, the pillar represents a highly stylized human form. One theory holds that Nevali Cori served as a religious center for a tribe already organized into a hierarchy of chieftains, priests, hunters, farmers, and tradespeople.

In the photo below, the ruins of the temple—viewed from above—include a niche in front of which worship may have been conducted. The hole in the floor marks the site of a second limestone pillar that modern looters tried to remove; in doing so, they smashed it to bits.

The back of a cult statue's head displays what may be a snake or a ponytail. The face is gone, having either eroded away or been vandalized. The sculpture, fixed into the temple wall, came from a statue apparently used in an older, surrounding structure.

A man and woman extend their arms heavenward on this fragment of a limestone bowl, perhaps as the participants in a ritual. Between them is a round figure that has been identified as a Euphrates turtle, a possible symbol of fertility; some scholars, disputing this, see the shape instead as a roly-poly baby. The bowl itself may have been employed in ceremonies: The inside displayed blackening, as though it had been used for holding a fire or burning incense.

Ashikli Höyük
AN ASTOUNDING PRECOCITY

Ashikli Höyük, dating to 8000 BC, offers one of the oldest examples in Anatolia of a developing village. Although the inhabitants still sustained themselves largely by hunting game and collecting plant foods, they led a settled existence. More than 150 buildings made of mud brick have been uncovered. As seen in the photograph below, these structures stood close together, often with only the narrowest of passages between them. Since no doorways on ground level have been uncovered, Ufuk Esin, the Turkish archaeologist excavating the site, assumes that entry must have been through holes in the roof, with ladders for access.

The inhabitants followed a burial custom common to other Neolithic sites in Anatolia, that of interring their dead under the floors of their houses. Most of the females faced north, most of the males south. All the bodies were buried with their knees flexed in a fetal position. The ages of the adults ranged from 18 to 57. Even the young showed evidence of traumatic arthritis and dental disease.

Walls of closely packed houses and workshops in Ashikli Höyük lie framed by the archaeologists' balks. Typically, houses had ovens and low mud-brick dividers demarcating living spaces; a few had firepits and ovens. Floors and interior walls were plastered smooth and some were painted pink, red, and yellow. One structure painted red may have been a temple.

The skull above, of a 20- to 25-year-old
mother who was buried with her infant,
provides startling evidence of the world's
first known brain surgery. She had suffered
a back injury; a seed-shaped hole in the
cranium made by a drill, perhaps to relieve
pressure, can be seen in the photograph
(above, right) of the back of her skull.

A necklace, reassembled from polished pieces
of agate recovered from a female's grave at
Ashikli Höyük, reveals an early taste for
adornment. The necklace is made up of
beads pierced lengthwise by a drill. While
eight of the beads are whole, two were broken and have been repaired. All were carefully smoothed around the holes.

Chayönü
BOLD STEPS FORWARD

Though some farming went on at Ashikli Höyük, substantial evidence of agriculture's beginnings—and effect—comes from Chayönü. There, American and Turkish archaeologists excavating between 1963 and 1988 under the direction of Robert J. Braidwood of the University of Chicago's Oriental Institute and Halet Cambel of Istanbul University discovered that the inhabitants had raised lentils, peas, and wheat, and—at a later point in Chayönü's development—sheep and goats.

Active from about 7250 to 6000 BC, the community—which like others in Anatolia had not yet learned to make fired pottery—took several giant steps forward. Among these was the use of metal. The inhabitants heated local copper to soften it, then hammered it into such practical items as hooks and pins. In addition, they were among the world's first formal architects, employing a rudimentary form of measurement and even limestone cement to lay a floor in which they embedded chips of salmon-colored limestone.

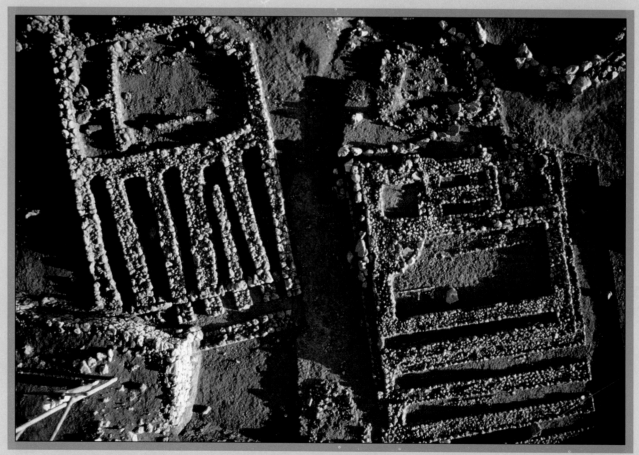

Two so-called grill-plan buildings at Chayönü display a kind of air conditioning—conduits laid in parallel rows under the floors. These may have facilitated the circulation of fresh air, preventing the buildings from becoming damp in winter—and perhaps keeping stored grain from molding.

Viewed from above, the so-called skull building at Chayönü (left) held the mysteriously charred tops of more than 90 skulls in two of its three antechambers. Apparently used for communal functions, the 26- by 23-foot structure is one of the oldest nondomestic buildings ever unearthed. In the large chamber lay a one-ton, well-polished stone; analysis of its surface and a large flint knife found nearby turned up residues of human, aurochs, and sheep blood.

Perhaps the head of an idol, this flat bone disk (below) from Chayönü has what appear to be eyes shedding tears. The four lines at the top may represent hair. Through the mouth a thong was likely threaded later so that the piece could be worn as a pendant. The flat bottom could have been attached to the idol's body.

A stone button and a copper bead point to some of the basic strides made at Chayönü. Although agriculture apparently required more hours of labor than the hunting-and-gathering way of life, the winter season gave farmers time to devote to the production of necessary items and the development of crafts. Some may have gone on to become specialists.

The world's oldest known piece of cloth still clings, in semifossilized form, to the antler handle around which it was wrapped at Chayönü some 9,000 years ago, possibly to provide a better grip. The fabric is believed to be linen, woven from locally grown flax.

Chatal Höyük
A CITY OF ACHIEVEMENTS

The agricultural revolution that ushered in a new way of life for humankind came to bear abundant fruit at Chatal Höyük, one of the world's first true towns. Its inhabitants raised cattle, goats, and sheep, as well as wheat, barley, and several other edible plants; they were manufacturers and traders in addition. And in time, they took another step forward; they began producing fired pottery.

To have developed a complex urban society like theirs, the people of Chatal Höyük must have exhibited a high degree of cooperation and cohesion. As excavations have shown, they had an involved religious life, engaged in various crafts, and made impressive artistic contributions— not least of which were the paintings decorating the walls of their houses or shrines. The paintings first began coming to light in 1961 when Chatal Höyük's original excavator, British archaeologist James Mellaart, stripped away the dust and detritus of the intervening millennia, even removing layers of plaster, to get at them.

The remains of Chatal Höyük's houses reveal the pueblolike construction typical of the city. Based on the size of the one-story structures—each taking up about 30 square yards—and the size of the city, archaeologists estimate that the population numbered between 5,000 and 10,000 souls, the limit of the agricultural area's carrying capacity for crops and livestock.

36

A wall relief (left) from what is believed to have been a shrine, reconstructed in the Museum of Anatolian Civilizations at Ankara, may depict a stylized woman giving birth. Beneath the form is one of several plaster bull's and ram's heads that decorated the chamber. Some 40 shrines from nine occupation levels have been excavated in Chatal Höyük. Religion appears not to have existed separate from daily life; rituals were carried out close to home—perhaps even at home.

A bearded man with his hair parted in the middle—some scholars see him as a god, maybe even the consort of the mother goddess—rides what seems to be a bull in the stone carving above. Male statues are much less numerous than female ones in Chatal Höyük, suggesting a society fascinated with fertility and reproduction.

Hunters surround a stag in this mural from a building in Chatal Höyük. Of the frescoes on the walls, some show humans and animals, others geometric designs. All reflect a high degree of artistry. In several, vultures hover above headless figures on the ground, perhaps the dead laid out for scavengers to strip off flesh. Curiously, many of the paintings had been covered over with plaster; in one house, with more than 120 coats.

THE THUNDER OF A THOUSAND HORSE-DRAWN CHARIOTS

On an archaeological treasure hunt in the Syrian city of Hama in 1872, the Irish missionary William Wright and the British consul at Damascus, W. Kirby Green, seemed fated to meet with nothing more than exhaustion and discouragement. The two had journeyed to the city, which they knew by its biblical name, Hamath, in search of ancient blocks of basalt, including one that the Swiss explorer Johann Ludwig Burckhardt had discovered but not removed some six decades earlier. Chiseled with rows of enigmatic hieroglyph-like symbols, it had escaped serious scrutiny until 1871, when the American consul general in Syria published a painting of a similar stone, one of five that he found in Hama. The blocks had since acquired considerable renown; antiquities dealers, in fact, had offered the townspeople large sums for one of them. But the Hamathites, believing the inscriptions on the blocks harbored a magical cure for rheumatism, jealously kept them hidden. When quizzed on their whereabouts, "all whom we asked," said Wright, "looked us steadily in the face and swore vehemently that there were no stones such as we sought in Hamath."

The conspiracy of silence held until Wright and Green at last happened upon a man who confessed to having one of the relics embedded in the walls of his house. After that, Wright declared, "we had no difficulty in finding all the stones." Gratified with the turn of

Relic of a mighty people long lost to history, a silver rhyton, or libation cup, in the shape of a bull represents the Hittites' principal deity, the weather god. Its placid expression, however, belies the power of the Hittites, who at one time posed a major threat to the Egyptians.

events, the pair showed the artifacts to Sub-hi Pasha, Syria's Turkish governor, whom they had accompanied to the city on an official visit, and he immediately ordered the blocks cut free.

News of the magistrate's command outraged city residents. Within hours, they took to the streets, swearing oaths to destroy the holy stones rather than see them removed. The pasha was obliged to post sentries at each of the sites throughout the night to ensure that the blocks survived until morning, when the work of transporting them was to commence. As it turned out, the soldiers more than earned their keep, for the effort was herculean: Dragging the largest stone to temporary safe storage in the governor's compound one mile away required no less than 50 men, four oxen, and the entire day. According to Wright, the block's laborious trek "kept the city in an uproar" until nightfall.

Then, with the blocks finally in the governor's possession and an agitated crowd milling in the streets, a meteor shower lighted the skies over Hama. At first the Syrians took the display as a sure sign of Allah's displeasure, an evil portent of things to come if the stones were not returned to their rightful places. But the governor calmed their fears by proclaiming that since no one had been hurt by the falling stars, the omens were good. They indicated the "shining approbation of Allah" for the loyalty of the Hamathites in delivering the precious stones into the hands of their "beloved Khalif, the Father of the Faithful." With these words, what had been an occasion for panic suddenly became a cause for celebration.

Wright and Green, however, wasted no time reveling. Having promised to deliver the blocks to the Istanbul Archaeological Museum, they instead set to work making two plaster casts of each of the inscriptions. One they sent to the British Museum, the other to the Palestine Exploration Fund. Now, it was hoped, scholars could

This sphinx from Hattusha's Sphinx Gate, dating to about 1230 BC, and the bronze statuette of a god at right, produced sometime between 1300 and 1200 BC, give some impression of the vanished Hittites' appearance. The shared features include high cheekbones, a square jaw, pronounced eyes, and large ears.

begin the important work of deciphering the mysterious characters. As to who had carved them, Wright already had a theory: The inscriptions, he later wrote, "would show that a great people, called Hittites in the Bible, but never referred to in classic history, had once formed a mighty empire in that region."

Wright based his supposition on a handful of references in the Old Testament to the Hittites, one of several peoples the Israelites found inhabiting Palestine when they arrived in the Promised Land. Most of the allusions involved shadow figures who vanished almost as quickly as they were named in the text: It was "Ephron the Hittite," for instance, who sold Abraham the cave in which he laid the body of his dead wife, Sarah. Similarly, it was the nameless "king of the Hittites" who bought horses from Solomon, who in turn is said to have counted Hittites among his many wives.

Had it not been for another fleeting reference in chapters 6 and 7 of 2 Kings, Wright might have written off the Hittites as just another of the forgotten peoples of Palestine. The passage tells of how the king of Syria amassed a vast army and laid siege to the capital of the kingdom of Israel, in time reducing its citizens to a starvation diet of ass's heads and dove's dung. But then, just when the beleaguered townspeople were abandoning all hope, a miracle occurred: The Lord "made the army of the Syrians hear the sounds of chariots and of horses, the sound of a great army." Believing that the king of Israel had summoned the combined forces of the Hittites and the Egyptians to his defense, the Syrians fled in terror.

Certainly an army capable of inspiring such panic—indeed, a military force given equal billing with that of the Egyptians—could not have been mustered from an inconsequential tribe of desert nomads. If the Bible was to be trusted as a historical document—and Wright had implicit faith in its veracity—then the Hittites had been a prodigious power, one that could have left its annals chiseled on the stones of Hamath.

Others were not so sure. Earlier, a noted 19th-century scholar had criticized the biblical passage for its "unhistorical tone," and the majority of historians apparently still agreed. Not one offered a more plausible theory. Thus, for lack of a better term, the stones' curious hieroglyphs were styled simply as "Hamathite."

As it turns out, such inscriptions were not limited to ancient Hamath. Almost at once, other Hamathite writings were recognized: at Aleppo, 75 miles to the north; near Ivriz, in south-central Turkey;

at the ancient trade center of Carchemish on the Euphrates River at the Syrian-Turkish border. And in fact, a rich trove of Hamathite had already been found among the remains of a citadel near Boghazköy (a village now known as Boghazkäle) in central Turkey's windswept highlands, 90 miles east of Ankara.

There in July 1834, the French archaeologist and adventurer Charles-Félix-Marie Texier came upon the peculiar-looking characters, and he encountered more of the inscriptions about a mile away, on the walls of the limestone outcrop known to the locals as Yazilikaya, or "Inscribed rock." Texier was certain that the citadel and rock sanctuary with their singular hieroglyphs were not of Roman origin, but he could not say what other ancient civilization might have spawned them.

The pedigree of the Boghazköy and Yazilikaya inscriptions would remain a mystery for four decades. Finally, in 1879, the British philologist Archibald Henry Sayce noticed that two or three of the hieroglyphs shown in published photographs of Texier's findings matched those on the stones of Hama and Carchemish. To Sayce—who had begun reading Homer in Greek at the age of 10—the script's widespread distribution suggested the existence of a common civilization, if not a nation. But not until Egyptian and Assyrian writings came to light referring to a mighty people dwelling in a land called Hatti did Sayce identify the writers of Hamathite. These could be the Hittites of the Bible, compatriots of King Solomon and the Israelites, scourge of the Syrian army.

And so in 1880, before a packed meeting of the Society for Biblical Archaeology in London, Sayce declared again what the Irish missionary William Wright had written six years before: that the Hamathite inscriptions were the handiwork of a people called the Hittites, whose power and reach had been grossly underestimated by modern historians.

This time, the assertion met with praise as well as criticism. Wright—to whom, after all, some of the glory for rediscovering the Hittites properly belonged—offered no complaint. On the contrary, he produced the first book on these long-lost people, *The Empire of the Hittites*. Though riddled with assumptions that would in time prove false, the book pioneered the new study of Hittitology and changed forever the way historians viewed the ancient world. The Hittites—speaking, as it were, through their as-yet-indecipherable script—had at last begun to reclaim their rightful place in history.

Majestic in repose, a stag forms the body of a Hittite silver rhyton (right, above). Encircling the cup is a scene (right) depicting a dead stag (near right), intended as an offering to the seated goddess or to the god standing on the back of another stag (center). A text found in Hattusha described this deity and called him the God Who Protects the Fields; in similar texts, he is the "Protective Deity." So precious were these vessels of silver—and gold—that they often were bestowed as gifts on foreign heads of state. It was recorded that "one vessel of silver in the shape of a stag" was presented by Shuppiluliuma I to an Egyptian pharaoh.

Over the ensuing century, Hittitologists would reveal a civilization far older than the one first glimpsed by Wright and Sayce. The Hittites of the Old Testament—known to present-day historians as the Neo-Hittites—were but the cultural descendants of far more glorious forebears *(pages 49-51)*. While perpetuating many earlier practices, the Neo-Hittites postdated the actual Hittites by as much as five centuries and ruled only the southeast periphery of the former Hittite realm in modern northern Syria and southeastern Anatolia.

The empire from which the Neo-Hittites took their name got its start some 1,700 years before the Christian era—and not in Syria as Sayce had surmised, but in the rugged highlands of the central Anatolian plateau at Boghazköy, the site of Texier's rambles. Though the French explorer could not have realized it at the time, the ruins he beheld were those of the Hittite capital itself, a place the ancients called Hattusha.

Built in stages over hundreds of years on a rocky promontory between two precipitous gorges and ultimately surrounded by double walls topped with half-timbered brick battlements with windows and crenelated turrets for archers, Hattusha during its heyday in the 13th century BC covered 414 acres. Excavations conducted there by a number of archaeologists,

and especially by the Germans Kurt Bittel and his successor, Peter Neve, have revealed not only an imposing citadel that served as the residence of powerful warrior-kings but also a broad adjoining district that was home to an unfathomable number of temples in which those rulers gave praise to gods, major and minor.

Commanding troops drawn from allies and vassals as well as from their own people, who lived in villages and cities outside Hattusha's walls, over the centuries the Hittite leaders rumbled forth from this combination stronghold and temple city to conquer much of the Middle East. Through their conquests they built an empire that at one time stretched from the Black Sea south to the plains of Syria and from the Euphrates River west to the shores of the Aegean Sea. And they did not quake in the face of their enemies' power. Dashing deep into Mesopotamia aboard revolutionary, light, spoke-wheeled chariots pulled by teams of swift horses bred in the Anatolian highlands, Hittite soldiers early on altered the course of history by sacking Babylon and bringing Hammurabi's fabled dynasty to its close. Centuries later they would clash swords with another great army, checking the might of Ramses II of Egypt. Though the weapons Hittite warriors wielded in these battles were made of the metal befitting their time in history—the Bronze Age—artisans back home were among the first in the world to master the more demanding craft of smelting iron ore. Hittite kings, in fact, made gifts of the iron jewelry—more desirous than gold—and other specialty items their blacksmiths produced.

Yet for all their power and expertise, the Hittites disappeared suddenly around 1200 BC, leaving few obvious traces of their former grandeur but an extraordinary wealth of documents, most in the form of inscribed clay tablets. Since 1905, some 25,000 have been unearthed among the ruins of Hattusha, including more than 3,000 that Neve recovered from a single royal archive in 1990 and 1991. When, after decades of archaeological detective work and painstaking trial and error, scholars finally understood how to read some of the texts, they learned of a civilization marked not only by a genius for militarism and administration but also by a remarkable religious tolerance. The Hittites, tablets reveal, left the shrines of their enemies standing and did not meddle with local cults, which they permitted to remain independent. Instead of replacing the various deities, the Hittite kings strove to enhance the local gods' importance and even traveled annually from one cult center to another, celebrating major

A WOMAN'S SEAL OF APPROVAL

Women in Anatolia in the second millennium BC had advantages that the women of Egypt and Mesopotamia could only imagine. Equality guaranteed by law allowed them to pursue professions held elsewhere only by men. But the best example of parity is in the royal house, where the queen ruled jointly with the king—and often, it would seem, independently.

Clay tablets reveal that this balanced partnership existed in central Anatolia from the beginning of the second millennium to perhaps the end of the Hittite empire, about 1200 BC. Even though only titles appear in the early documents, they show that queens were empowered to rule autonomously. In the period of the Hittite empire—the 14th and 13th centuries BC—identities of queens become quite evident, particularly on clay seals where their titles and names have been incised either with those of kings or alone. The one queen, however, for whom a wealth of documentation has been uncovered—including the joint seal above right—is Puduhepa, powerful wife of Hattushili III and mother of Tudhaliya IV.

Although Puduhepa may not have had any more duties than her predecessors, she did

44

festivals. By empire's end, when a state religion seems to have been created out of the many local cults, the deities of the Hittite pantheon numbered 1,000. To this multifarious host they turned in earnest prayer whenever, as one Hittite scribe wrote, "things get too much for a man."

Of course, gaining such insight into Hittite culture remained only a dream at the end of the 19th century, when the discipline of Hittitology was still in its infancy. The world had at last acknowledged the existence of the Hittite empire, but where it was centered and what its curious hieroglyphs conveyed remained tantalizing mysteries.

As with the rediscovery of the Hittite civilization itself, the solution to these conundrums would follow in part from chance finds. Of these, none was so influential as a cache of clay tablets discovered in 1887 near Tell el-Amarna, a village on the Nile River 200 miles south of Cairo. The tablets, each one covered with neat lines of cuneiform, turned out to be part of the diplomatic and administrative correspondence of the great pharaoh Akhenaten, who had his capital, called Akhetaten, constructed at the site in the 14th century BC. Many of the tablets contained references to an illustrious "King of Hatti" and detailed the movements of his armies. One tablet had even been written by a Hittite monarch, King Shuppiluliuma, who in courtly fashion congratulated the young Akhenaten on his ascension to the Egyptian throne.

The majority of the letters were written in Babylonian Akkadian, the diplomatic lingua franca of the day. Two, however, were in an unknown language that scholars referred to as Arzawa, after the king of Arzawa, who wrote one letter and received the other. Clues as to who might have spoken such a tongue came in short order. First, near Boghazköy in 1893, the French archaeologist Ernest Chantre acquired the fragments of two cuneiform tablets that also turned out to be written in Arzawa. Then, in 1905, a piece of clay tablet from Boghazköy inscribed with Arzawa came into the hands of the German Assyriologist Hugo Winckler. With that, the effort to identify the speakers of Arzawa took on a new impetus.

Winckler and a team of assistants descended upon Boghazköy in October intent on unearthing more of the tablets. An unexpected onslaught of the rainy season limited their campaign to three days,

reign in an era when the empire was at its zenith and a long-tenuous relationship with Egypt—and Ramses II—was steadied with the famous Treaty of Kadesh. Cut into a silver tablet, the treaty bore the stamp of Hattushili on one side and that of Puduhepa on the other.

Years later Ramses accepted two daughters in marriage from the Hittite monarchs, further solidifying the alliance between the two great nations. Letters from the pharaoh to Puduhepa indicate the respect he accorded the queen; in them he refers to her familiarly as "my sister."

For all her queenly duties, Puduhepa must have been well-loved by her son Tudhaliya IV: The legend on a seal impression reads "son of Hattushili and Puduhepa." It is the only known example of a royal seal that names Puduhepa as the king's mother.

Looking more decorative than practical, these vessels served a ritual purpose—the dispensing of wine, oil, or honey for the gods. The design of the curved, beaklike spout on the 16th-century-BC pitcher above continued in use for centuries. The pitcher opposite, from the 14th century BC and found in Hattusha, would have been used for libations as well, but its shape suggests that it represented continuity, perhaps the annual cycle, or even infinity.

but it proved spectacularly successful nonetheless: Winckler turned up 34 clay artifacts, most of them in untranslatable Arzawa. The tablets, along with the vast dimensions of the Boghazköy ruins, seemed to him to mark the site as a Hittite stronghold; perhaps Arzawa was the language of the Hittites. To find out, he determined to return the following year.

This time, Winckler and his party arrived in July, well before the seasonal rains. They set up their headquarters tent on the rock mass known as *Büyükkale,* or Big Castle, the location of Boghazköy's citadel, and concentrated their search on the western slope and the plain beneath it. A specialist in ancient languages, Winckler devoted no thought to systematic archaeological technique; unearthing and deciphering tablets was his only concern. Ludwig Curtius, an assistant, watched as the foreman—a "handsome, lanky young Kurd by the name of Hassan"—uncovered a neat row of perfectly preserved clay tablets. "The Kurd attacked them as casually as a peasant woman digs potatoes out of her field," Curtius noted. Then he tossed them into a basket for Winckler, who awaited the harvest in a wattle hut nearby.

To protect against flies and to "ward off the overpowering interest the friendly little animals took in my work," Winckler had to cover his head and neck and put on gloves, despite the fierce heat of the Anatolian summer. As he pored over the tablets, many of which proved to be written in readable Akkadian, it soon became obvious that Boghazköy was no ordinary settlement. "That it had been a great center was now quite clear," Winckler wrote, "and that it could not be the remains of the archives of an insignificant king was also definite." But what relation the ruins bore to the Hittites and to the unknown land of Arzawa, Winckler could not yet say.

The answer was not long in coming, however. Approximately 20 days into the dig, an assistant brought Winckler a beautifully preserved tablet written in Akkadian *(page 68)*. "One look at it," Winckler recalled, "and all the experiences of my life paled into insignificance." What his eyes beheld was the text of a letter from Ramses II, pharaoh of Egypt, to Hattushili III, king of the Hittites, describing the terms of a historic peace treaty between the two superpowers and former enemies. The compact itself, already known to Winckler virtually by heart, had been inscribed in Egyptian hieroglyphs 3,100 years before on the walls of the temple at Karnak and the pharaoh's mortuary temple, the Ramesseum, on the west bank of the Nile opposite Thebes. And now here was a letter—undoubtedly the basis upon which the final treaty was drawn—setting out word for word, paragraph by paragraph, "in the most beautiful cuneiform script and good Babylonian," the same agreements and conditions as the famous Egyptian versions.

Such a letter could have come only from the archives of the great Hittite kings; Boghazköy, then, must have been the capital of the Hittite empire. As for the land of Arzawa mentioned in the Tell el-Amarna letters, later investigations would show that it had been a vassal state of the Hittite realm, where, of course, "Arzawa"—or Hittite—was the official language.

In three additional years of excavation at Boghazköy, Winckler unearthed some 10,000 tablets and fragments. From the many written in Akkadian, he was able to ascertain the names and exploits of a scattering of Hittite kings, thereby laying the foundation for an eventual reconstruction of Hittite history. But by far the greatest number of tablets—those written in the Hittite cuneiform—remained stubbornly mute until Bedrich Hrozny, a brilliant Czech professor of Assyriology, made them yield some of their secrets.

A specialist in ancient Semitic languages, Hrozny could not make sense of the Hittite words per se, but he could read the wedge-shaped characters with facility. Working phonetically, he singled out what seemed to be proper names. Then he moved on to identify ideograms—that is, word pictures—borrowed directly from Babylonian cuneiform, the script from which the Hittites' own written tradition had developed.

One such ideogram was *ninda,* meaning "bread." Hrozny encountered it amid a string of untranslatable terms in the sentence *nu ninda-an ezza-teni vadar-ma ekutteni.* As he studied the forms of the individual words, he played with an audacious idea originally proposed in 1902 by the Norwegian scholar J. A. Knudtzon—that Hittite exhibited grammatical structures characteristic of the Indo-European family of languages. These tongues, including those of India, central and western Asia, and most of Europe, are believed to have originated from the same source sometime before the dawn of recorded history.

The notion flew in the face of everything scholars of Middle Eastern history believed. Yet the more Hrozny pondered

47

his *ninda* sentence, the stronger his conviction grew. The Hittite word *ezzateni*, for instance, bore an uncanny resemblance to the Old High German word *ezzan*, meaning "to eat." And what, Hrozny asked, do you do with *ninda*, or bread? You eat it! Then there was the Hittite *vadar*. Phonetically, it sounded like the Old Saxon *watar*, the English *water*, and German *Wasser*.

Like pieces of a puzzle, the meanings of the words tumbled into place. Relying on intuition honed by years of linguistic study, Hrozny ventured a translation of the sentence: "Now you will eat bread, further you will drink water." It was a moment of pure illumination in which he felt, as one journalist put it, "that shudder of awe which voices from immemorial tombs evoke."

Hrozny could scarcely wait to share his extraordinary insight. On November 24, 1915, he stood before an assembly of the Near Eastern Society in Berlin and proclaimed Hittite to be an Indo-European language. Predictably enough, the declaration elicited scorn, but Hrozny paid his critics no mind. On the contrary, he went on to publish an exhaustive study of the grammatical structure of Hittite, and in 1919 he brought out the first lengthy translations of the Boghazköy tablets.

Though it would take the collaboration of many philologists to unravel the tangled skein of the Hittite tongue, Hrozny's seminal work made possible the first tentative glimpses into the vast Hittite archives—one of the oldest libraries in history. Only now, with the enigmatic code of Hittite cuneiform at last broken, could the Hittites begin to shake off the dust of time that for so long had obscured them from scholarly view.

Still, a small portion of the Hittite annals remained inaccessible: those texts, like the mysterious Hamathite inscriptions, that had been rendered in Hittite hieroglyphs. Archibald Sayce had made headway in translating six of the hieroglyphs by the end of the 1880s. Some of these were deciphered when he found a so-called bilingual—a silver seal with inscriptions in both Hittite hieroglyphs and cuneiform in a known Hurrian dialect. But a real breakthrough would not come until 1946. That year Helmuth T. Bossert, a professor at the University of Istanbul, discovered inscribed slabs flanking the twin entrances to a Neo-Hittite fortress at Karatepe, in the Taurus Mountains of southern Turkey. In each instance, the panel to the

HEIRS TO THE HITTITE NAME

Charles Texier and William Hamilton unknowingly explored the cradle of the ancient Hittite empire in central Anatolia as early as the 1830s. But it was not until other scholars came upon "Neo-Hittite" artifacts later in the century in southeast Anatolia and Syria, and tied them to the earlier discoveries, that the once-lost empire was rescued from oblivion.

The Neo-Hittites were not true descendants of their namesakes. They were in fact eastern Anatolians and Arameans. Around 1000 BC, two centuries after the Hittite empire collapsed, these groups constituted a loose organization of states that lasted until 700 BC, when the neighboring Assyrian empire annexed their realms and turned them into provinces. They were known as Hittites because they occupied former Hittite cities and took many aspects of Hittite culture, including the language, as their own. For their art and sculpture, they resorted to traditional Hittite forms, such as carved rock reliefs, and altered these with elements of their own Syro-Mesopotamian culture. The result of such artistic crossbreeding is seen in the ninth-century-BC relief of the thunderbolt-bearing weather god, Teshub *(left)*, found in Babylon. To this adopted Hittite god, with his distinctive short tunic, upturned boots, and conical hat, the Neo-Hittites added slight Assyrian touches, most notably the style of, and attention to, the god's curly beard.

Such reliefs alerted scholars to the possibility that a Hittite nation once flourished in Anatolia. But the Neo-Hittite artifacts did more than just prove that the legendary "men of Hatti" were real. Their inscriptions left archaeologists a record of the post-imperial history of the Hittites. And the fact that strains of Hittite culture persisted five centuries after the empire's collapse—and as far east as Babylon—testified to the Hittites' former dominance in a region once thought to have been just the backyard of the Babylonian, Assyrian, and Persian empires.

This fragment of a lion gate (above) from a Neo-Hittite summer palace near Carchemish, built at the end of the eighth century BC, shows how Assyrian influence came to prevail as Neo-Hittite power eroded. All but the guardian lion, an old Hittite motif, is Assyrian in expression.

A young Hittite girl, holding a falcon in her left hand and a writing tool in her right hand, perches on her mother's lap in this ninth-century-BC relief from southeastern Turkey. Neo-Hittites favored domestic scenes over those of war and statecraft—evidence that they led a relatively peaceful and contented life before being overtaken.

Rare for their domestic charm, these three panels (below), complete with accompanying hieroglyphic inscription, depict the reigning king of Carchemish and his family. The prince (far left) leads the monarch on his arm, while the queen trails, holding a baby and pulling a goat. The divided middle relief shows other, presumably royal children at play as well as a toddler taking his first steps.

right was carved with Hittite hieroglyphs, while the panel to the left bore Phoenician in a readable Semitic script. Because the content of each was nearly identical and the text was lengthy, scholars were able to use the inscriptions to compile a working vocabulary and grammar for Hittite hieroglyphic. Thus, nearly seven decades after Wright and Sayce first rediscovered Hittite civilization, historians finally held the dual keys to the Hittite kingdom.

The solution to the longstanding riddle of how to read the Hittite texts drew scholars' attention to an altogether different enigma: If the Hittites indeed spoke an Indo-European language—that is, one that was not indigenous to the Anatolian plateau—then where did they come from?

Hrozny, who believed he detected traces of the western Indo-European language group in the structure of the Hittite language, proposed that the empire builders originated in the west. Others argued that the Indo-Europeans descended from an ancestral home in southern Russia. And to this day, scholars remain divided on the issue. The route by which the newcomers made their way to the cen-

Aloft in the gondola of a hot-air balloon in 1993, German archaeologist Peter Neve pauses in the filming of Hattusha, 4,900 feet below. For Neve, aerial photography added another dimension to archaeology. Although the elevation tended to flatten the terrain, it did provide a complete view of the city's layout and its construction. Just as important was the opportunity to record any unusual bump or depression—unnoticeable at ground level—for further investigation.

tral Anatolian plateau—either from the west, across the narrow strait of the Bosporus, or from the east, after passing between the Black and Caspian Seas and over the Caucasus—also cannot be described.

The discovery of an indigenous settlement beneath a later Indo-European town at Alaca Höyük, about 15 miles northeast of Boghazköy, has led historians to surmise that the wanderers reached Anatolia sometime before the 19th century BC—but exactly when, and whether they came en masse or in a trickle, is unclear. What is certain is that the native populace they encountered—the Hattians—would in time combine with them and the Hurrian people of southern Anatolia and northern Mesopotamia to form the Hittite civilization. Indeed, the word *Hittite* is derived from the name of the Hattians' homeland—Hatti.

The earliest direct evidence of an Indo-European presence in Anatolia comes from the ancient city of Kanesh near Kayseri, about 95 miles to the southeast of Boghazköy. Hrozny in 1925 revealed that the Assyrian traders who established a *karum*, or merchant colony, at Kanesh around 1950 BC kept meticulous cuneiform records of all their transactions, including loans and contracts. Among the many Hattian customers listed on the thousands of clay tablets were a scattering of names with Indo-European elements. From these, archaeologists assume that the Hittites had begun to make their mark by the 19th century BC.

Significantly, the city that would one day be their capital—Hattusha—also appears on tablets as the residence of a number of the Kanesh merchants' business partners. And indeed, Kurt Bittel's excavations at Boghazköy confirmed that a sister karum existed at the site. Digging at the base of Büyükkale, he distinguished several historical phases, the oldest of which corresponded to a pre-Hittite Hattian settlement. The Assyrian karum lay on its northwestern outskirts and appears to have postdated Kanesh by a century or so, having probably formed sometime around the 19th century BC.

Both the karum and the Hattian city burned to the ground in the late 18th century BC, as a

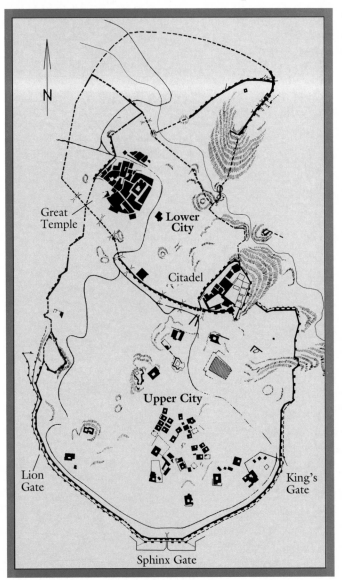

In the drawing below, the well-fortified city of Hattusha takes shape from its excavated remains. Substantial amounts of the wall foundations survive and are defined with a solid bold line; random traces are mapped out with a broken line. In the northwest, the Great Temple complex dominates the Lower City, while the Citadel in the east—distinguished by its royal palace and archives—sits isolated on its plateau. The carefully planned Upper City, with its gateways and multitude of buildings, was, according to Neve, a "temple city." It was constructed by Tudhaliya IV and his son Shuppiluliuma II in the last few decades of the 13th century BC, before the empire collapsed and Hattusha was destroyed.

Great Temple

Lower City

Citadel

Upper City

Lion Gate

King's Gate

Sphinx Gate

N

heavy blanket of charred debris and rubble found by Bittel attests. Were it not for several copies of a text preserved in the royal archives of the Hittite palace, historians would have little clue as to what befell the unfortunate traders and town residents. The document—purportedly copied by a Hittite scribe around 1700 BC from a stone monument erected outside the gate of an Anatolian city-state—chronicles the deeds of two kings, Pithana and his son Anitta. They are credited with having conquered not only Kanesh (where a dagger or spearhead bearing Anitta's name has been found) but, more important, the karum and town at Hattusha. "I took it by storm in the night," Anitta is quoted as saying, "and where it had been, I sowed weeds. Whosoever becomes king after me and again settles Hattusha, may the Storm God of Heaven strike him."

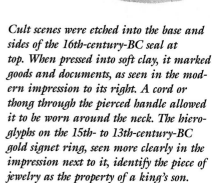

Whatever the Hittites thought of this bellicose conqueror, they clearly ignored his curse. More than a century after Anitta sacked Hattusha, the Hittite king Hattushili I rebuilt the city and made it the capital of his realm. The first known Hittite ruler, a murky historical figure thought to be either Hattushili's father or his uncle, had pushed the kingdom's borders south to the shores of the Mediterranean and west into the tiny kingdom of Arzawa. And now Hattushili, every bit the warrior-king his predecessor was, marched his armies southeast across the Taurus Mountains and toward Aleppo in northern Syria. Along the way, he took the ancient city of Hashshu, which "he overwhelmed like a lion with his paw," exults a cuneiform text chronicling Hattushili's exploits. "Dust he poured on it and with its possessions he filled Hattusha. Silver and gold knew neither beginning nor end."

Cult scenes were etched into the base and sides of the 16th-century-BC seal at top. When pressed into soft clay, it marked goods and documents, as seen in the modern impression to its right. A cord or thong through the pierced handle allowed it to be worn around the neck. The hieroglyphs on the 15th- to 13th-century-BC gold signet ring, seen more clearly in the impression next to it, identify the piece of jewelry as the property of a king's son.

Glorious as such victories were, they did little to ease Hattushili's search for a successor, for at some point in the king's reign, scholars know, he found the heir to the throne, his nephew, plotting to depose him. Outraged, Hattushili went before an assembly of nobles and delivered a speech, known as his Political Testament, that archaeologists found recorded in the state archives at Boghazköy. In it, Hattushili decried the conspiracy, exiled the schemer, and named his grandson, Murshili I, heir to the throne. Then, addressing Murshili in particular, he offered advice for the kingdom's safekeeping: "You must keep my words!" he warned. "As long as you keep them, Hattusha will stand tall, and you will make your land be at peace. . . . If you do not keep them, your land will pass under foreign control. Give careful attention to the words of the gods! Their sacrificial loaves, their libations, their cakes and their flour must always be set up. . . . My son, what is in your heart, do always."

Murshili seems to have heeded his grandfather's advice, for under his governance, the Land of Hatti grew considerably. In the mid-16th century BC, having first conquered northern Syria, the young king pressed his armies some 500 miles down the Euphrates to Babylon. There, in a feat of miraculous daring, he laid the storied city to waste. Afterward, his attention diverted by news of political unrest at home, he abandoned the capital and withdrew to Hattusha.

Like Hattushili, Murshili was not permitted to bask in the glow of his triumphs. Shortly after his return, he was murdered by his brother-in-law, Hantili, and Hatti plunged into a dismal interlude of palace intrigue and internal strife that lasted several generations. One by one, the kingdom's hard-won conquests broke away, and its status as an international power waned. According to the archaeologist Peter Neve, it is to this period that Hattusha's first great wall belongs. He located the stone foundations of a 26-foot-thick defensive wall with projecting towers that encircled the Citadel and the adjoining residential district. Under the very real threat of invasion, the city was transformed into a grand fortress three-quarters of a mile long and a quarter mile wide.

Ironically, however, it was to take much more than a rampart to save the ailing Hittite kingdom, which teetered on the brink of anarchy—it would require yet another palace coup. In 1465 BC, Telipinu, the consort of a royal princess, seized the throne and, with a single-mindedness that was to characterize his later reign, disposed of all his rivals in one bloody stroke. He then issued an edict delineating—for the first time in Hatti's history—precise laws of hereditary succession. Carefully preserved in the Hittite archives, the regulations were, with a single exception, faithfully observed down to the closing days of the Hittite empire.

Telipinu's decree also made clear that, even though the king was the supreme ruler, his actions were at all times subject to

55

the scrutiny of the so-called Pankus, a ruling body of nobles. On this point, the law was unequivocal: It required those who sat in the Pankus to remind a king that "whoever commits evil among brothers and sisters" must answer for it "with his royal head."

A spirit of fair play distinguished the whole canon of Hittite law, whose formal codification, not unexpectedly, seems to have taken place during Telipinu's reign. Diggers at Boghazköy unearthed many fragments of clay tablets probably dating to the following century on which 200 laws of the land had been inscribed. The statutes—each framed in the context of a hypothetical case followed by a ruling—legislated the handling of everything from arson and rape to the theft of a beehive.

Scholars have remarked both on the Hittite kings' penchant for regulating all aspects of daily life and on the relative humanity of the laws. Unlike other codes of the time, they eschewed cruel punishments and emphasized restitution over retribution. "If a freeman sets a house on fire," reads one ruling, "he shall rebuild the house." Similarly, under Hittite law, if a person committed an act of murder, reparation was made to the victim's family by the killer. And women and slaves, though subordinate to freemen, were still accorded substantial legal rights. A widowed mother who was a landowner, for instance, could disinherit a son who failed to support her in old age, and a slave could own property. The compulsory death penalty for a freeman was reserved only for instances of rape, bestiality, and failure to comply with state authorities.

From the thousands of legal texts and title deeds retrieved so far at Hattusha, historians have pieced together a fair impression of what life was like for the average Hittite during the later part of the second millennium BC, when most of those who lived near the capital had their homes outside the city walls. Scholars know, for example, that the majority of citizens made their living on the land, husbanding livestock and cultivating edibles such as barley and emmer wheat. The land deed of the freeman and farmer Tiwatapara—only one of countless others like it—is typical. He lived in "the town of Hanzusra," probably a densely populated farm village, with his wife Azzia, his son Haruwanduli, and his two daughters, Anitti and Hantawiya. At the time his holdings were inventoried, Tiwatapara owned 22

For 200 years a remarkable and profitable trade system existed between Anatolia and Mesopotamia. In 1950 BC, Assyrian merchants established at least 10 permanent *karums,* or trade colonies, in eastern and central Anatolia. From the karums, donkey caravans transported gold, silver, and copper to the Assyrian city of Assur and returned laden with textiles, clothing, perfumes, and tin, essential in the production of bronze.

Crafts flourished in the karums; among the items produced are the ceramic animal-shaped ritual vessels below, which dispensed libations for the gods, and the pair of ceramic boots above, whose upturned toes became a signature of Hit-

tite dress several centuries later.

One commodity that the Assyrians gave Anatolia was priceless: the knowledge of writing. At Kanesh—the network's central and largest karum—excavations turned up thousands of cuneiform clay tablets revealing not only merchants' transactions but also letters written by Hattians, the native inhabitants, shedding light on their religion and lives.

But just as important is the name of another karum in the merchants' documents. Although destroyed along with Kanesh, it would later rise from the ashes as Hattusha, the capital of the Hittites.

sheep, 18 goats, five kids, four lambs, six draft oxen, and two other oxen. He held one acre of meadowland in the town of Parkalla for pasturing his oxen and three and a half acres of vineyard on which he grew 40 apple trees and 42 pomegranate trees.

If his goats wandered into his neighbor's vineyard and browsed, the law obliged him to pay for every acre they damaged and specified that restitution be made in silver, the medium of exchange throughout the Near East at the time. The metal, which was exchanged in the form of rings and bars, was measured in shekels, a unit of weight the Hittites borrowed from the Babylonians. And should Tiwatapara decide to hire out his draft oxen to supplement his income, all he could legally charge was one shekel a month. According to the code's official table of prices, this take would not have gone far: To buy a single cheese for his dinner would have cost him half a shekel. And a "fine shirt" to wear at table—three shekels more. Life in the Land of Hatti was neither easy nor cheap, it seems.

Not everyone eked out a living on the land, of course. Hittite records, including a petition signed by guildsmen protesting their temporary conscription into state labor, have provided scholars with a roster of Hittite occupations, among them stonemason, merchant, physician, scribe, basketmaker, cobbler, weaver, potter, and priest. No less than farmers, such artisans and professionals were subject to the dictates of the king—which on occasion included being drafted along with prisoners of war to do the hard work of empire building.

It was presumably on the backs of such men that a renovation of Hattusha was undertaken beginning in the 14th century BC, perhaps to repair damage caused by an attack of the Kaska, a fierce, nomadic tribe that inhabited the lands directly to the north. Over the period of a century or more, the Hittite capital was transformed from a provincial town into a city worthy of being touted the seat of an empire. The old burg of 160 acres—comprising the Citadel and the adjoining residential district—more than doubled in size, advancing upslope and south on either side of two wide valleys. To the existing compass of city wall, Hittite engineers added a colossal extension to make a four-mile-long circuit of towering breastworks surrounding the sprawling capital.

A chance find made in 1957 has given archaeologists a clear vision of the former grandeur of the fortifications. Excavators digging west of the Citadel uncovered the fragments of a large ceramic storage jar that dated to around the 14th century BC and that was shaped like a tower flanked by parapets with rounded crenelations. At the top of the tower were narrow windows—certainly replicas of the openings through which Hittite archers may once have kept vigil over the outlying countryside.

At least seven major gates offered passage through the outer wall. Soaring arches buttressed by guard towers, the passageways supported enormous doors of bronze-covered wood that opened onto well-defended gate chambers. According to a directive from a Hittite ruler named Arnuwanda—scholars cannot say for sure which of the three kings with this name issued it—an elaborate protocol governed the opening of the mammoth portals. The text was addressed to the *hazannu*, a government official charged with Hattusha's security. "You, Hazannu," it reads, "be very careful in matters of the guard. . . . When they lift the copper bolts on the gate in the morning, . . . when you have sent your son or servant to open the doors, when the seal on the gate turns, then afterward a man from Hatti or a commanding officer, or whoever is on duty, shall together examine the seal at the gate and open the gate accordingly."

The same security measures were repeated at the entrances to the Citadel, itself girdled by prodigious fortifications. Here, as the excavations of Bittel and Neve showed, the flurry of urban expansion begun in the 14th century BC had also left its mark: Monumental royal buildings connected by narrow, covered walkways and opening onto three courtyards—at least one of which was bordered by a colonnade—gradually replaced the modest edifices of earlier days, and a cult area complete with an artificial pond was constructed on the Citadel's southern rim.

Bittel and his team of archaeologists determined that the king's private apartments lay in the lofty northernmost corner, a privileged station commanding magnificent views of the mountainous countryside in three directions. Though excavations yielded little, investigators have some inkling of what the royal quarters were like thanks to the discovery of instructions recorded for the benefit of palace personnel. In these texts attendants are reminded each morning to draw

With its chains intact, this bronze tablet was recovered in 1986 less than 100 feet west of the Sphinx Gate. The text concerns a state treaty between Tudhaliya IV, son of Hattushili III, and Tudhaliya's cousin, Kurunta of Tarhuntassa, who vied with Tudhaliya for the crown. Tudhaliya's warning—"If you lay claim to the throne in Hattusha, may you and your sons be destroyed by the gods!"—must have gone unheeded. Clay seals of the weather god and sun goddess, once affixed to the chains to legalize the treaty, were not found, indicating removal prior to the tablet's deliberate burial. This would have nullified the agreement.

the curtains of the king and queen's apartments, which are described as containing a throne, an offering table, and a hearth. Also mentioned are a dairy, pantry, kitchen, and toilet.

Immediately southwest of the royal residence Bittel's excavators unearthed the remains of a building that must have stood at least two stories tall. On the basis of its imposing size and grand design—traces of the first-floor wall partitions suggest the one-time presence of an overlying story graced by 25 wooden pillars—the German architect Rudolf Naumann proposed that the structure was a royal audience hall. A corridor connected the hall to the main palace archive, where Bittel found thousands of clay tablets tumbled from what once had been an extensive ladderwork of wooden shelving. Mixed among the debris were rectangular or oval clay labels three inches long. Apparently they provided Hittite researchers with a guide to the shelves' contents; on one label was written "Tablets concerning the deeds of Murshili."

By far the greatest number of clay tablets were devoted to religious matters, reflecting a preoccupation with the metaphysical that is echoed in the city's many shrines. To date, excavators have turned up the remains of 31 temples in Hattusha, ranging from natural rock outcrops to elaborate formal structures, and Neve believes there probably were many more, especially in the high ground at the southern end of the city *(map, page 53)*. Ceremonial access to the temple district was gained via three symmetrically arranged, grand gates whose names derive from the images that Hittite sculptors carved to adorn them: in the east, the relief of a deity or king; in the west, lions; and in the south, on the highest land in the city, sphinxes.

Noting that the king is positioned on the inside of the gate and that the lions are on the outside, while the sphinxes face both in and out, Neve proposed that the trio of gates may have served as way points for some kind of sacred procession. The participants, he says, likely moved from east to west: Departing the Upper City through the King's Gate, they followed the city wall to the Sphinx Gate, where they reentered the temple district. Then, moving single file, the marchers made their way out once again through a long, dark tunnel beneath the gate, walked to the Lion Gate, and entered the Upper City for the last time. Though the exact purpose of the procession can only be guessed at, archaeologists have discovered fragments of a clay tablet that might offer a clue. The pieces contain instructions for a religious ceremony in which a Hittite god in the form of a cult image is removed from a temple, placed in a ribbon-festooned chariot, and paraded in the company of torch-bearing dancers and temple prostitutes to a special house in the woods.

Many temples were constructed during the expansion that began in the 14th century BC: more than 20 in the Upper City and a major one in the old city center. The latter, known to scholars either as Temple 1 or as the Great Temple, is the largest and best preserved of the grand sanctuaries. Comprising a number of buildings, the complex rambled over some five acres and was divided by a ceremonial thoroughfare that ran northwestward from a main entrance in the south. To the east of the street, foundation blocks of limestone signaled the location of the temple proper, a rectangular structure with an open-air courtyard at its heart. A battery of narrow storerooms surrounded the sanctuary on all four sides. Similar buildings on the west side of the street seem to have served as an administrative center where office clerks and scribes once busied themselves with inventorying the temple's treasures and more than 200 other service personnel, including priests, musicians, and singers, lived.

A tablet recovered from one of the temple's eastern storerooms in 1962 has so far provided archaeologists with the only clue to the identity of the gods worshiped there. It details the creation of a gilded statue of silver fashioned in the shape of a bull and dedicated to the weather god of Heaven and the sun goddess of Arinna, the supreme divinities of the Hittite state and the two most closely identified with its military fortunes. It was to them that the king turned

Reassembled and standing almost three feet tall, this pair of 14th-century-BC terra-cotta bulls (left) served as libation vessels. An opening at the base of the neck allowed for filling, with the contents decanted through the nostrils. Excavations of the Citadel in 1963 recovered the fractured figures (above) from a large circular hearth in a deserted sanctuary. They are representations of the sacred bulls—Sheri and Hurri, or Day and Night—that pulled the weather god's chariot and served as intermediaries between the deities and earthly supplicants. No longer useful, they had been ritually buried.

in times of battle and emergency. According to instructions preserved in the royal archives, temple priests feted the deities' golden statue daily, solemnly offering fruit, wine, olive oil, and bread, as well as the occasional yearling lamb. To fail in such devotions was to imperil the welfare of the entire Hittite realm.

The raising of the Great Temple—like the grand remodeling of Hattusha itself—coincided with a period of unprecedented conquest in Hatti's history. In 1343 BC, King Shuppiluliuma I ascended the Hittite throne, commencing a reign that would catapult Hatti from kingdom to empire in 20 short years. The transformation was to come, as in the Bible stories of old, with the thunder of a thousand horse-drawn chariots, whose every move—successful and otherwise—was scrupulously chronicled by Shuppiluliuma's son.

As had the lawmaker Telipinu more than a century before him, Shuppiluliuma assumed the reins of power only to confront a realm hurtling toward ruin. The trouble this time came not from within, but from the slow encroachment of external foes who now pressed the kingdom from all directions. After first shoring up Hattusha's defenses—the prodigious extension of the city wall was built at his behest—Shuppiluliuma focused his energies on subduing the greatest of Hatti's adversaries: the powerful kingdom of Mittani, some 300 miles to the southeast in northern Syria. Though the first campaign, in 1342 BC, failed, the king regrouped and went on to claim a resounding victory only six years later.

In 1334 BC, Shuppiluliuma led his battle-hardened forces back across the Euphrates on a whirlwind conquest that netted Hatti seven Syrian vassal states. Now only a few cities stood between the Hittite king and his dream of total dominion over the lands to the southeast of Hattusha. Among them was Carchemish, the Anatolian city-state that controlled a major trade route at a ford in the Euphrates River. Masters of siege warfare, Shuppiluliuma's troops encamped outside the ancient entrepôt and, sustained by a baggage train of pack asses and ox-drawn wagons, beleaguered it for seven days. After a "terrific battle" on the eighth, Carchemish fell.

An incident that occurred during this foray betrays something of the repute enjoyed by the ruler among the courts of the Near East at the time. The story, recorded in the Hittite annals, was first discovered by Winckler in 1906. It tells of how Shuppiluliuma, resting

Tiny images of Hittite gods, as seen here, may have been personal votives or pendants. It is unknown what the gold figure (top left) represents, but the peaked cap and the curved staff classify him as a god. The gold 15th- to 13th-century-BC seated deity (bottom left), wearing a disk-shaped headdress—symbolic of the sun—and holding a child, is said to be the sun goddess of Arinna, wife of the weather god. Hattushili III's queen, Puduhepa, concerned about Hattushili's health, offered prayers to the goddess in return for "long and enduring years and days" for her husband.

in his tent outside Carchemish, received a messenger from Egypt. To the king's surprise, the emissary carried a letter not from a pharaoh, but from a queen. "My husband has died," the message read, "and I have no son. But of you it is said that you have many sons. If you would send me one of your sons, he could become my husband and a king for the country of Egypt."

Suspicious but keenly aware of the strategic benefits to be had from placing his scion on the throne of Egypt, Shuppiluliuma dispatched his private secretary "to find out what truth there was in the matter with the woman." Many scholars have long thought that the queen in question was the widow of Tutankhamen, but some now argue that she may have been Meritaten, the daughter of Akhenaten and Nefertiti, and the wife of Smenkhkare, Akhenaten's immediate successor. After receiving another letter from the queen expressing impatience and indignation at the Hittite sovereign's foot-dragging, Shuppiluliuma finally sent a prince. But it was too late: In the meantime, another dynasty had already taken the throne, and the young bridegroom, perhaps the victim of assassins, disappeared before reaching his destination.

Fortune seems to have turned its back on the great empire builder, for in 1322 BC, Shuppiluliuma himself died, a victim of the plague brought back by his armies from northern Syria. Nevertheless, he bequeathed to his sons Arnuwanda II and Murshili II, Arnuwanda's successor, a realm nearly 300,000 square miles in extent, stretching from the Aegean Sea in western Anatolia south to the mountains of Lebanon and eastward from the Mediterranean all the way to northern Iraq.

Though a shrewd military commander and politician, Murshili was a deeply troubled man. Afflicted with a severe speech impediment since his youth, when he was struck by lightning, he believed himself accursed of the weather god. Worse, the pestilence that had killed his father was spreading throughout the realm. Anxiously, he consulted the oracles to learn the cause of his ill fortune. The answer came back: The king was paying for a sin committed by his late father. Failure to atone for it through earnest sacrifice would result not only in his own ruination but in that of Hatti as well. The warning seems to have made such an impression on Murshili that he never missed an opportunity to render tribute to the gods. In fact, the annals report that he returned to Hattusha from a distant campaign just to celebrate the spring *purulli* festival honoring the weather god.

63

Upon his death in 1296 BC, Murshili passed on to his son, Muwatalli II, an empire whose holdings rivaled those of imperial Egypt. In fact, the distant outlands of the two empires actually touched south of the Syrian city-state of Kadesh on the Orontes River, in a region that previously, in the glory days of Egypt's 18th Dynasty, had paid tribute to the pharaohs. But as Ramses II, the ambitious third ruler of the 19th Dynasty, ascended the Egyptian throne, he pledged to oust the Hittite pretenders and reestablish Egyptian hegemony over the coastal region of the eastern Mediterranean.

In the fifth year of his reign, the pharaoh launched his offensive against the Hittite-held territories. Muwatalli's response was immediate and overwhelming. Egyptian records report that the Hittite king "gathered together all countries from the ends of the sea to the land of Hatti" and marched south with some 40,000 soldiers to meet his challengers. The result was a clash of historic proportions involving two of the mightiest armies in all of antiquity.

The battle, fought around 1275 BC on the plains near Kadesh, ended in a draw. Afterward, the two armies—each claiming victory—withdrew to their strongholds. Years of cold war followed, during which internal political strife once again plagued the Hittite empire. Upon the death of Muwatalli in 1273 BC, Hattusha was rocked by the first coup d'etat since the days of Telipinu. Muwatalli's brother, Hattushili III, usurped the throne of his nephew, the son of a royal concubine, and sent the boy into exile—gestures for which the conscience-stricken king would later offer elaborate justification, as the Hittite annals record.

History, however, would remember Hattushili not for his villainy, but for his shrewd statecraft. In 1259 BC, 16 years after the Battle of Kadesh, he concluded the extraordinary peace treaty with Ramses II of Egypt by which each side pledged not to attack the other and to come to the other's aid in the event of attack by a third party. Securing the agreement was a feat of skilled diplomacy requiring lengthy negotiations between several members of both ruling families. Archaeologists have found no fewer than 45 letters pertaining to the treaty at Boghazköy—the most famous being the clay tablet unearthed by Winckler in 1906. Consummate statesman that he was, Hattushili cemented the fragile coalition in 1246 BC by sending his eldest daughter to wed Ramses, who subsequently commemorated the event with a carving on the south side of the temple at Abu Simbel. Though badly weathered, the relief still shows two splendidly

YAZILIKAYA: A SHRINE HIDDEN AMONG THE ROCKS, AWAY FROM PROFANE EYES

About a mile from the Hittite capital of Hattusha is one of the world's most unusual shrines—Yazilikaya, or "Inscribed rock." Here naturally carved passages winding between giant stone outcrops served as the inner recesses of a temple.

Built on top of rubble, the temple probably rose just one story high, as seen in the drawing at right. Its flimsy construction, as evidenced by the surviving ruins, suggests to scholars that the temple's use was limited to special occasions, perhaps when the king and queen—as chief priest and priestess—celebrated the festivals of spring and autumn.

The rites may have inspired reliefs on the walls of the larger gallery, Chamber A, depicting 66 gods and goddesses—males to the left, females to the right—marching toward the end of the hall where the principal deities meet. This heavenly assemblage seems to reflect the Hittite belief that the fertility of earth and livestock depended on the deities convening in the house of the weather god at the beginning of the new year. The relief of a king—whose cartouche identifies him as Tudhaliya—stands apart from the rest, perhaps in his capacity as high priest.

The smaller Chamber B seems unaffiliated with the larger chamber. Its entrance is protected by two lion-headed, winged demons, and the reliefs and niches within have led scholars to think it may have been a mortuary for dead kings.

Yazilikaya dates to the mid-13th century BC, during the reigns of Hattushili III and his son Tudhaliya IV. Although the deities would be recognizable to anyone from Hattusha, the hieroglyphs are Hurrian. When Puduhepa, Hattushili's Hurrian queen, arrived at Hattusha, her people's deities were integrated into the Hittite pantheon.

The drawing below shows one wall in Chamber A occupied almost entirely by male deities, with the exception of the Hurrian goddess of war, Shaush-ga (second from right), *and her two attendants. Most of the gods have been identified; the 12 crowded figures at the end of the line, however, remain unnamed. Chamber B has 12 similar gods* (detail at left), *but no one knows whether they are in fact the same deities as seen in Chamber A.*

A detail (left) *from the relief at the end of Chamber A, where the primary deities confront each other, shows the Hattian weather-god entering from the left astride the bent necks of mountain gods as he greets his wife, the sun goddess of Arinna, and their son Sharruma, both of whom stand on the backs of panthers. Above the double-headed eagle emblem on the right are the sun goddess's daughter and granddaughter.*

In Chamber B (right), *King Tudhaliya IV is depicted in the protective embrace of his patron god, Sharruma, who is seen in the relief on the right. The niche next to them—one of three—may have held the king's cremated remains. The relief on the left is of a half-buried sword: Its hilt forms the bodies of two lions, its pommel the head of a god. According to a Hittite ritual text, resident gods of the underworld were re-created by priests in the image of swords, which were then secured in the ground. These reliefs—and 12 armed gods on the opposite wall—strongly indicate that this was, as German archaeologist Kurt Bittel pointed out, "a temple of the dead."*

in response to a warning from a neighboring monarch that raiders were approaching by sea.

Many historians find it hard to accept that the seafarers—thought to be a mix of Philistines, Sicilians, Sardinians, and other groups from the coast of Asia Minor—shattered the Hittite realm single-handedly. Instead, they subscribe to the view that other marauders, perhaps the Kaska tribes, may have been involved, and that internal enemies had to play a part as well. Indeed, among the last chronicles filed in the archives of Hattusha was a text attributed to a scribe of Shuppiluliuma II complaining of dissension and rebellion within the empire: "The inhabitants of Hatti sinned against His Majesty," the writer laments.

It has been suggested that this dissatisfaction may have stemmed not from any political clash but from famine and malnutrition brought on by a force that all Middle Eastern peoples were powerless to combat—climatic change. Indeed, historians know that in the three centuries following the time of the Hittite collapse, weather conditions throughout the region were warmer and drier than in the 300 years that went before. Though seemingly trivial, such a trend may in fact have been disastrous, and especially so for a people whose fortunes were tied to animals and crops that in the past had been watered by seasonal rain and melting snow. That people in other lands probably experienced similar hardships and, like the Hittites, set off in search of greener pastures, may only have compounded the pervasive misery.

For most of this arid period, history recorded nothing of the once-proud Hittites. Then, around 1000 BC, 15 petty kingdoms arose on Syria's northern periphery. They used Hittite hieroglyphs, but some of them spoke an unrelated tongue. Though not empire builders, these Neo-Hittites found life beyond their mortal years in the pages of the Old Testament and, more important, left behind the clues that centuries later led to a rediscovery of the grander civilization.

STRONGHOLD OF THE HITTITES

Even from the vantage point of temple ruins high on a plateau in Hattusha *(above)*, the capital of the Hittites, the view of the surrounding hilly countryside fails to convey the immensity of the imperial city that once loomed there. Covering 414 acres, with a circumference of four miles, Hattusha is difficult to envision, and because of the irregular landscape, it is almost impossible to photograph in its entirety.

The ruins in this picture lie in the Upper City, a religious precinct at the southern end of the capital. In the background can be seen the remains of several other Upper City temples. To the right and well below those temples—but not visible because of elevation—sit the ruins of the Citadel and its royal palace, which occupied the highest point in Hattusha's older section before construction of the Upper City. Farther away and to the northwest are the extensive foundations of the Great Temple, the setting for some of the Hittites' most important ceremonies.

These and other remnants of Hattusha's imperial past have been brought to light by archaeologists and scholars over the years. Charles Texier's discovery of the site in 1834 eventually led to the unearthing by Hugo Winckler of the first archive of cuneiform tablets in 1906. In 1907 the joint expedition of the German Oriental Society and the German Archaeological Institute, under the codirectorship of Winckler and Otto Puchstein, began large-scale digs. But the excavations did not become systematic until 1931, when Kurt Bittel took over. His student Peter Neve, who began working with Bittel in 1954, took up the directorship in 1978. During his tenure, Neve—who retired from active, on-site work in 1994—completed excavations of the Citadel and Great Temple, then turned his attention to the still-unexplored Upper City.

The next several pages present fleeting images of the once-great capital. With the aid of archaeologists, Hattusha is slowly regaining some of its lost grandeur.

THE HOME OF THE HIGH AND MIGHTY

Hattusha's rocky, fissured terrain was put to use in building its defenses. Outcroppings were incorporated and towers built on top of them; ramparts filled in low-lying ground, presenting a stony and presumably insurmountable face. Towers broke the major wall's battlements at 100-foot intervals, and sets of heavy doors made gates secure. Parallel walls ran around the southern rampart. Perched on high ground and backed up to a ravine, the Citadel, where the king lived, was encircled by its own wall; another cut across Hattusha's midsection, dividing the Upper and Lower cities.

The walls—26 feet thick in some places—surely gave the citizens a sense of well-being. But no matter how impregnable these might have seemed, they could not keep out the enemy, and Hattusha fell about 1200 BC. Evidence of remodeling-in-progress at the Sphinx Gate indicates that the end was as unexpected as it was sudden.

Created with earth removed from the inner city, then faced with stone, this rampart wrapped around the more vulnerable southern end of the Upper City. Most of the original facing was discovered intact, with only a few areas requiring restoration over the primary substructure. Cut through the embankment, a 236-foot-long, corbel-arch tunnel runs directly under the wall and into the city above.

More than eight feet tall, this limestone sphinx and a mate were found in fragments at the inner gate of a small chamber of the aptly named Sphinx Gate. Because the Sphinx Gate was centrally located in the Upper City's wall and at Hattusha's highest point, it has been suggested that the gate was not a conventional portal but served as a processional gate and sanctum.

Found in Hattusha in 1957, the fragment above from the rim of a 14th-century-BC clay vessel lends veracity to the 1907 drawing below of a section of the Upper City's fortifications. Crenelation on the tops of the walls and towers and vertical openings in the front and sides of the towers gave clear advantage to sentries and archers.

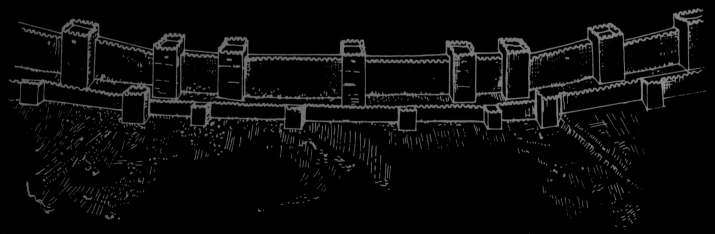

At least seven gates pierced the outer wall and five that of the Upper City. Chief among those in the newer section were the well-preserved and well-adorned King's Gate in the southeast *(right)*, the Lion Gate in the southwest *(lower left)*, and the Sphinx Gate, which was situated between the two.

The thick, double-casemate walls lent themselves ideally to the portals' structure: box-shaped guardhouses with enormous carved blocks that formed parabolic arches; solid wooc bronze-plated doors at each enc flanking towers overhead. Ev. dent still are the sockets and th holes for bolts and crossbars.

From a palace archive a cla tablet reveals instructions fo opening and closing the gates. I speaks of copper bolts, and it de scribes the "turning"—or break ing—of seals first thing in the morning, probably a device tc detect any unauthorized entry after the gates had been securec for the night.

Excavated in 1907, lions guard the entrance to the Lion Gate. Carved from huge blocks that served as doorjambs, only the beasts' forequarters protrude from the stones, giving the illusion of either sitting or standing, possibly the sculptor's intention. More important, perhaps, is the integration of the animals into the total structure, which may well be a Hittite innovation.

Minutely detailed to include even chest hair and nail cuticles, the 7½-foot King's Gate god emerges from limestone in high relief.

Erected in 1967, a plaster cast of the original god figure keeps vigil inside the King's Gate. After vandals had all but destroyed the feet of this copy, officials raised the ground level to prevent further destruction. The original, removed by Turkish conservator Theodor Makridi in 1912, was stored until it could be displayed in a museum of Anatolian treasures that opened in 1932 in Ankara.

A 1907 sketch of the exterior of the King's Gate shows a small portion of the intricate meshing of huge mortarless blocks, and a corbel-arch entry. Executed with the city's defense in mind, the design included stone walls on both sides of a long, narrow ramp, limiting wheeled traffic, such as war chariots, to a single lane, as did the inclusion of a sharp turn, or angle.

THE GREAT TEMPLE: A CITY WITHIN A CITY

In the northwestern region of the Lower City, a complex of buildings and rooms sprawls across five acres of rough land. For decades, its identity remained unclear; many scholars thought it was a palace. Today, it is generally referred to as the Great Temple, the house of Hattusha's principal deities, the weather god and sun goddess. The reason it has been so designated is that several smaller buildings, both inside and outside Hattusha, conform to the sanctuary's divisions of gate, courtyard, pillared hall, and cella. What was once taken to be a throne's substructure has since been identified as the base for a large statue—long lost—that may have portrayed the weather god or sun goddess.

The other buildings in the compound served the temple's needs—that is, what the gods required—and housed the gods' servitors. Sitting on an artificial terrace, with paved streets and a protective wall, the complex was, in effect, a highly organized, self-sufficient city in microcosm.

The Great Temple not only catered to the needs of the gods but also was an archive and treasury. In storerooms in the north lay charred lumps of clay and labels that had seal impressions as well as obvious string holes to attach them to bags. The bags may well have contained deliveries and contributions to the temple from state officials and princes of the realm. Also discovered were the seals of two 13th-century-BC kings, Muwatalli and Hattushili III, and the latter's queen, Puduhepa.

A 1975 drawing of the Great Temple shows a complex of odd-shaped buildings intersected by streets. The squarish structure at near left was the sanctuary; large jars, containing tributes for the gods, were stored in the surrounding rooms. The long building at far left may have housed kitchens, bakeries, workshops, and offices.

Huge storage jars stand where they were when the Great Temple collapsed around them. Their contents remain a mystery but probably consisted of wine, oil, and grain, as part of the annual tribute to the weather god and sun goddess. Many vessels—the largest had a capacity of 793 gallons—were too large to pass through doorways, so the building was erected around them.

An ivory triad of deities was found in an Upper City temple in 1984. The central figure, wearing a bull mask, represents the weather god. The other two cannot be identified, but they display emblems of divinity—the typical conical hat and the kalmush, or curved staff.

PEOPLES
OF THE MIDAS
TOUCH

This 2,700-year-old ivory statuette, only 6 ½ inches tall, may represent the Phrygian mother goddess Kybele accompanied by her two children. She wears a high, cylindrical headdress over a long veil tucked into her belt—Kybele's characteristic attire.

From a distance, they look like conical hills—more than 80 of them. But an uninformed viewer coming upon them might wonder why they rise so abruptly from an otherwise flat landscape. The truth of the matter is that they are not natural but man-made—tumuli, piled up two and a half millennia ago by countless workers to hold the noble dead. And they are extraordinary. The tallest soars 170 feet on a broad base 980 feet in diameter, and deep within it lay hidden one of the most complete tombs ever found anywhere.

The tumuli stand on the flood plain to the east of the Sakarya River on the central Anatolian plateau, 55 miles southwest of Ankara. Between them and the riverbank is another landmark, known as Yassihöyük, or the "Flat Mound." The product of time—of a centuries-long cycle of building, destruction, and rebuilding—the mound contains remains dating from the Early Bronze Age all the way up to the Galatian and Roman era. Yet the principal reasons for the area's appeal to archaeologists are that Yassihöyük holds what is left of Gordion, the capital of the once-great kingdom of Phrygia, and that the nearby 170-foot-tall tumulus is believed by many experts to be the resting place of Midas. The last and best known of Phrygia's rulers, he inspired the myth about a king cursed with the ability to turn to gold everything he touched.

Among the scholars drawn to the region was the American archaeologist Rodney S. Young of the University of Pennsylvania. In the autumn of 1955, having worked on the site for five years and excavated 14 of the small tumuli, he was preparing to embark on a dig that promised to reveal much about the occupant of the largest one.

From his earlier excavations Young knew that each tumulus sheltered only a single tomb, a four-sided chamber built of wood, and that each of the mounds consisted of three layers: a pile of rubble, usually small stones, heaped around and on top of the tomb; an overlying, thin shell of clay, probably intended to hold the rubble in place; and a thick covering of hard-packed earth. He knew as well that the tombs were rarely located at the midpoint of the tumuli. Young suspected that the builders may have done this intentionally to hide the burials from robbers, but centuries of prevailing southwesterly winds may also have played a role, especially on larger tumuli, by distorting the mounds' shape through erosion. As a result, he recognized that digging down from the summit or blindly tunneling in from one side would be futile—and destructive. "This is the biggest tumulus in Asia Minor," he wrote, "a monument in itself and therefore not to be wantonly destroyed or mutilated."

Workers using a drilling rig make borings to determine the location of the tomb inside the tumulus known as the Midas Mound. With a diameter of approximately 980 feet and a present height of 170 feet, it is the biggest of the more than 80 tumuli at Gordion. The position of the burial chamber was detected when the drills hit the stone rubble used to surround and protect it.

So Young started his explorations by attempting to locate the rubble he expected would surround the tomb. Beginning at a point just above the southwest edge of the tumulus and moving methodically up the slope, he sank a series of test shafts using a lightweight oil-drilling rig. As the water-cooled bit chewed into the earth, he kept a close eye on the material it churned up and any resistance it met along the way; if nothing else, the drilling enabled him to chart the distance from the upper surface of the tumulus to the hardpan on which it rested. After several weeks of probing, he had failed to locate the tomb. Not until July of the following season did the probe strike telltale rock 112 feet beneath the top. Subsequent boring revealed that the rock belonged to a pile of rubble less than 100 feet in diameter, and more promising still, that the pile lay, as expected, just to the southwest of the midpoint.

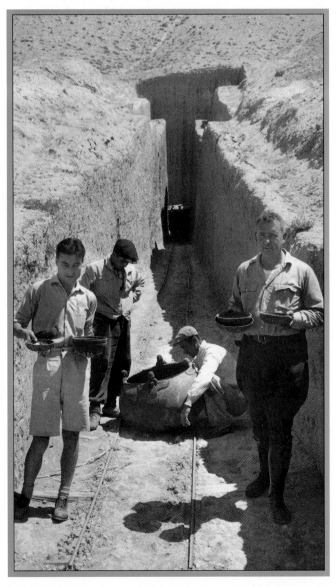

At the entrance of the trench leading to the Midas tomb, the American archaeologist Rodney S. Young (on the right), director of the excavation, and Burhan Tezcan of the Turkish Antiquities Service show off bronze bowls recovered from the burial chamber. The rail tracks at their feet were laid the length of the trench and the tunnel beyond it so rubble could be removed easily in coal wagons from the interior of the tumulus. Behind the men a Turkish worker squats beside a bronze cauldron.

In triumph Young planted a mast bearing a banner atop the tumulus at the spot beneath which he believed the center of the tomb would be found. Then, in April 1957, he and his team began to dig. Starting from the southwestern edge of the tumulus, they sank a narrow trench down to the level of the plain and moved inward, toward the point marked by the mast. As the excavators lengthened the gash, the earthen walls thus created grew higher. By the time the team had advanced about 230 feet, the vertical face before them loomed 38 feet tall. From here, the archaeologists would have to advance by tunneling.

Foreseeing the danger of a cave-in, Young had arranged to hire an engineer and professional tunnelers from the Zonguldak mining region, on the Black Sea. Their expertise, he hoped, would keep such a disaster from actually occurring. Working around the clock in three shifts and using only simple wooden props to shore up the walls, they advanced 10 feet a day. Twenty-four days later they reached a wall of rough limestone blocks that stopped them dead in their tracks.

The discovery took Young by surprise. He figured the miners were in the area of the rubble but had expected them to come up against a wall made of wood, not limestone. Could it be, he wondered,

The bones of a king—thought to be those of Midas himself—found in the tomb at Gordion enabled British scientists to take the skull and, using forensic techniques, reconstruct the monarch's features (above). *Scientists calculate the man stood 5 foot 2 and was 60 to 65 years old at death. The model is made of bronzed resin.*

that the tomb was built of stone? When the workers pierced the wall, which turned out to be about three feet thick, rounded rocks the size of oranges began tumbling forth. As fast as the men removed them, more poured out, and the stream kept up for three days, causing worries that the tomb's roof might have collapsed, allowing the rocks to smash flat whatever had been placed beneath it. Only after the workmen had carted away some 200 cubic yards of rubble were such fears finally allayed. There, about six feet ahead of him, Young saw another wall, this one made of trimmed but unfinished logs.

As the miners cleared the way to the wall's face, rocks fell occasionally from overhead. They had stuck to the clay dome, which Young was astonished and relieved to find intact. "Hardened and compacted by pressure in the course of time," he wrote, "it stood of itself when the stone pile, of which it was the mold, was withdrawn from underneath."

Cutting through the log wall, Young was startled to find more rubble behind it. Another four days would pass before the workers had removed most of the stones from the area, and at last Young stood before a second wood wall, this one constructed of carefully squared and fitted timbers. This, Young assumed, had to be the wall of the tomb chamber. He cut a small window into it. As he did so, the scent of sawdust filled the air, and he could hear a faint crackle coming from within the tomb as the air from the trench entered the ancient space and caused the dry and fragile wood inside to splinter.

The hole was big enough to allow Young to insert only his head, an arm, and a flashlight. "The staff took turns at looking in," Young wrote, recalling the excitement shared by everyone who tried to describe what they saw in the gloom. "The tomb was large, the atmosphere dense, the flashlight weak. Among the wonders thus seen were a chariot, and a stuffed alligator!"

The archaeologist made a saner appraisal of the tomb's contents later. The crackling sound, he realized, had come from the re-

82

mains of fine wood furniture—nine three-legged tables, two inlaid serving stands, and three ornamental stools. These had been preserved thanks to the clay dome, which had sealed out moisture and kept the chamber's humidity constant. Although the artifacts were in various states of collapse because of their antiquity, the mere survival of a material as perishable as wood was a rare bonus for archaeologists accustomed to dealing with pottery, stone, brick, and metals. Young immediately arranged for chemical treatment to save the fragments and still-whole pieces. Successful reconstructions of the furniture would be undertaken in the years to come *(pages 112-117)*.

Wood, however, was not the only material in which the tomb was rich. Ranged about the chamber were corroded objects of bronze. These included a large number of studs, thought to be the remains of showy leather belts, and 170 jugs, bowls, and other vessels, including ladles. The quality of their workmanship testified to a tradition of accomplished Phrygian bronzeworking, as did more than 180 intricate bronze fibulae, broochlike pins used to fasten clothing. Many of these lay scattered over the chamber's wood floor.

The most imposing pieces were three bronze cauldrons almost two feet tall and two and a half feet across, parts of which probably came from the eastern Anatolian kingdom of Urartu *(pages 91-93),* and two richly decorated bronze situlae—bucket-shaped ritual containers—that resembled vessels illustrated in late-eighth-century-BC Assyrian reliefs. Since stylistic analysis of the fibulae and radiocarbon dating of wood samples taken from the tomb's outer wall yielded similar dates, Young felt that the tumulus must have been erected around this time.

The most thrilling find, however, was located directly beneath and in front of the hole the archaeologist had cut in the wall. There lay what Young at first thought was a wood fourposter bed but later proved to be a coffin. On it rested the skeleton of the man for whom the entire monument had been raised. The rich objects buried with him, the date, the great size of the tumulus, even the man's age—determined to be between 60 and 65 by Muzaffer Senyürek, a paleoanthropologist at the University of Ankara—led the scholars to theorize that these were the bones of none other than Midas himself.

But if this was the storied ruler, a couple of mys-

In a fanciful illustration of the legendary King Midas from a 1910 book of Greek mythology, the monarch realizes when he touches his child and she turns to gold that the wish he was granted is a curse. Although the subject of many exaggerated tales, some dating to early Greek historians, King Midas was a real person, the Phrygians' most famous historical figure.

teries remained. Given Midas's mythical golden touch, why was his tomb not filled with gold? Searching the chamber thoroughly, the archaeologists were unable to turn up even a hint of the precious metal; nor did they find any of the weapons that were commonly placed in burials of early warrior-kings. Young speculated that it may not have been the Phrygians' custom to inter royalty with such items.

Also strange was the apparent anonymity of the tomb. Brief alphabetic inscriptions were found scratched into beeswax strips on three bowls. Young recognized the letters as Greco-Phrygian and knew that the inscriptions read from left to right, but he could not make sense of them. Thus firm identification remained beyond the grasp of those who wanted most to know who the man was. Nonetheless, the inscriptions proved that alphabetic writing had reached Phrygia by the last quarter of the eighth century BC and that the elite were not illiterate. These insights represented great advances for scholars, who previously had to rely on the records of the Phrygians' neighbors, the Assyrians and the Greeks, for information on how the people of Midas had emerged from the silent centuries that followed the downfall of the Hittite empire around 1200 BC.

The Assyrians referred to the Phrygians as the Mushki and Tabal, members of a troublesome federation of Anatolian peoples that was led by a king the easterners called Mita. According to the royal records of Sargon II, the Phrygians successfully resisted his plans to conquer their territory around 720 BC. The Greeks, who had commenced settling the Aegean's eastern islands and shorelines in the 10th and ninth centuries BC, believed that the Phrygians originated in the Balkans, fought on the side of the Trojan king Priam at the siege of Troy, moved onto the Anatolian plateau around 1200 BC, and in time came to rule it. Their dominance ended about 695 BC,

A delicately carved relief—captured here in an artist's rendering—remained visible on a furniture fragment that had been burned to charcoal. Brought to light during the excavation of Megaron 3 at Yassihöyük, the city mound at Gordion, the battle scene depicts a bowman on foot and warriors on horseback equipped with helmets, spears, and shields.

when the Cimmerians, invaders from the Caucasus region, overran their kingdom and Midas, tormented by bad dreams, is said to have committed suicide, supposedly by drinking bull's blood.

Greek writings relate that the Lydians, another people with a storied leader, ultimately took the Phrygians' place. Indeed, Croesus, the name of the most renowned Lydian king, became famous among the Greeks for his great wealth, as did Midas. And archaeologists excavating at Sardis, the Lydian capital, have discovered why: On the banks of the Pactolus, the mountain torrent on which the city stood, the Lydians had refined gold and silver and first introduced coinage.

But the Greek accounts of the Phrygians and Lydians were tangled with myth: Priam, for example, is said to have married Hecuba, the daughter of the Sangarius River, as the Sakarya—the stream that flowed past Gordion—was known in ancient times. Greek legend also tells that Midas's father, Gordius, bound his wagon with a sturdy knot to please Zeus Basileus, patron god of the oracle who had prophesied the Phrygian's reign. The so-called Gordion knot defied centuries of attempts to untie it, fostering the belief that whoever undid it would become the lord of all Asia. Though many tried, ac-

Turkish workers at Gordion carefully expose a mosaic floor resembling a crazy quilt in 1956. The freewheeling design surrounds a circular hearth that is only partially visible at this point in the excavation. Made from red, black, and white pebbles, the mosaic belonged to the main palace and dates from King Midas's time, the late eighth century BC.

A priest—hands clasped in a gesture of supplication that goes back to ancient Sumer—wears a headdress and pleated robe befitting his station in this hollow-cast silver statuette that stands five inches tall.

cording to historical tradition only one succeeded—Alexander the Great, who slashed it with his sword.

And in a famous story that linked the Phrygians' destiny with that of the Lydians, Midas supposedly won from the god Dionysus the gift of turning everything he touched to gold. Though at first the ruler rejoiced over his good fortune, he soon realized that his new power was also a curse, as he could not lift bread to his lips without rendering it inedible. Fearing starvation, Midas begged Dionysus to take back his gift, and the god complied. He instructed the ruler to wash away his "fault and its punishment" in the Pactolus, the river that runs past the Lydian capital. When Midas plunged into the water, his powers immediately passed to the river, and its sandy bottom—much to Croesus's eventual delight—became gold.

In more than 40 years of excavations at Gordion, Rodney Young and his American successors, Keith DeVries and G. Kenneth Sams, would do much to flesh out the earlier archaeological and mythological accounts. They would bare broad areas of Midas's splendid capital, whose pretension reflected his military ambition, and uncover evidence of the wealth that lay behind the myth of his golden touch. And despite the Greek historians' claims of close contacts between the Greeks and Phrygians—Herodotus wrote that Midas gave a wood throne to the shrine of Apollo at Delphi—the excavators would find only tantalizing hints of such links. Indeed, despite the expedition's success, the Phrygians would remain, in the words of one historian, "vague, amorphous, barbaric and mysterious."

The American excavations at the Phrygian capital marked the climax of a slow process of archaeological reconstruction that had begun more than 150 years before, when a British army captain, William Martin Leake, was traveling with his retinue in the craggy highlands near the present-day city of Eskisehir, west of Gordion. There he came upon a plateau on whose rocky face ancient stonemasons had hewed the facade of a houselike shrine with a gabled roof and a deep central niche suggesting a doorway *(page 114)*. Geometric designs covered it, along with inscriptions that Leake thought resembled an early form of the Greek alphabet; in one of these he saw what he took to be the name of Midas. Deciding that the monument had to be the work of the Phrygians recorded in Greek accounts, he grandly designated it the Tomb of Midas.

Modern scholars, of course, know the name to be inaccurate; they believe the monument is related not to Midas but to the practices of a water cult associated with the great Phrygian mother of nature, or mother goddess, Kybele. Nonetheless, Leake's account of his discovery launched a century of more-or-less-haphazard exploration of the highlands by a number of 19th-century European travelers. One of them, a British gentleman named W. M. Ramsay, surveyed and sketched remains demonstrating that the plateau where Leake had found the so-called Tomb of Midas was the location of a walled settlement that he called Midas City. Ramsay subsequently spent more than 12 years recording monuments that were recognizably Phrygian. In doing so, he revealed that the Phrygian realm encompassed much of the core of the previous Hittite empire and included even the old capital at Hattusha. Indeed, it and a series of modest walled towns built along trade routes far to the east testified to the Phrygians' occupation of the long bend of the Halys River.

The German archaeologists Alfred and Gustav Körte identified the mound of Yassihöyük as the site of the true city of Midas around the turn of the century. The spot was blessed with natural resources: The Sangarius River watered grazing land for sheep and horses, and there were plentiful supplies of timber for the construction of furniture such as Young found in the large tumulus. One of the American's earliest discoveries—an ancient paved road that ran nearby—seemingly gave an additional clue to Gordion's prosperity. Young thought it might be part of the so-called Royal Road, an east-west route connecting different regions of the Persian empire ruled by Darius I in the late sixth and early fifth centuries BC, but recent scholarship suggests that the two-lane artery was more likely a later Roman highway. But even if the road was Roman, it followed, as Young would determine, the line of older Hittite and Phrygian routes across the Anatolian plateau. Gordion grew up where these crossed the Sangarius, a most fortuitous location, ensuring Gordion a key role in Anatolian trade.

Hand in hand with such clues to the capital's rise, however, came evidence of its calamitous fall. Digging through Yassihöyük's many levels, the excavators soon came upon Phrygian buildings, all marked by fire. In some, large pieces of charcoal, the remains of wooden roof beams, littered the floor, covered by the feathery white ashes of the reed thatch that must have lain on top of them. In others, the Pennsylvania team found evidence of daily life brutally interrupted: a vase of hazelnuts placed in a workshop as snacks for laborers; chaff scattered over a threshing floor; the skeletons of two tethered, slaughtered cattle with their leg joints removed (the butchers were evidently at work jointing the beasts when disaster struck); and sewing kits standing ready for the textile workers whose fame would be recalled in the Latin word for an embroiderer, *phrygio.*

This spouted beer jug, standing only four inches high, is a fine example of Phrygian ceramic ware, generally characterized by its burnished surface and geometric designs in brown paint. The unusually long spout—from which the Phrygians drank—has a sieve, necessary for filtering the thick, grainy beverage. Relatively rare, such jugs are found only in royal tombs.

As the archaeologists laid bare more of the city, they could see that the conflagration had touched almost all of Gordion and realized that it would have been nearly impossible for such a fire to have spread so far without the assistance of arsonists. The excavators came to this conclusion after they discovered internal walls—thinner than the city's outer defensive circuit—that Young surmised were erected to divide the city into three discrete zones, perhaps to assist in the control of slaves. One was the so-called bastion area. A second held workshops where textiles were produced and food prepared. The third, which had particularly fine buildings and yielded telling finds, probably was the home of the Phrygian royal palace.

The fiery end fit well with the Greek version of Phrygian history. The ancients related that it was the Cimmerians who swept down into Anatolia and sacked Gordion. Though victorious, the raiders were apparently not bent on conquest, for they did not take over Phrygia. Rather, they moved on, settling in the Crimea, on the north edge of the Black Sea. Students of the Greek accounts estimate the invasion came around 695 BC, and pottery Young uncovered among the charred remains at Gordion squared with the date.

Curiously, the excavators turned up no sign of wholesale slaughter of the residents, just the debris left by the blaze sealed under a thick layer of clay. Shortly after the attack, evidently, the survivors had returned to the site and, intent on rebuilding, filled in the ruins to provide a platform for new construction. In doing so, they made it possible for the archaeologists to distinguish Midas's Gordion from the confused stratigraphy that characterizes Yassihöyük's other layers. The picture was clearest in the palace zone.

There Young discovered a complex of houses standing among paved courtyards. Though he came across few valuables, he could tell that this had been a capital worthy of Midas's kingdom. Two of the structures resembled Mycenaean Greek and Bronze Age Anatolian megarons—that is, houses featuring a large main room almost 30 feet square with a hearth and an adjoining, shallow foreroom. The stone walls of one such megaron measured six feet across and possessed regularly spaced niches, evidence that heavy timbers once supported the walls and roof.

The building must have had a splendid appearance: Smooth clay plaster coated the walls, and all the rooms were paved with mosaics of black, red, and white pebbles set in a bed of clay. No overall pattern governed the designs; rather, playful geometric shapes—swastikas, lozenges, interlocking triangles, large rosettes—appear scattered at random. Young remarked that the effect was similar to that induced by an oriental rug and suggested the transfer to stone of ancient weaving skills and designs.

The scale of the buildings led the archaeologist to believe that they had a public, rather than private, function, and unlikely evidence appeared to support his conclusion. Outside one of the megarons, Young found a low, wide bench made of stone and covered with mud stucco. From it, he in-

A 15-inch-high ceramic ceremonial vessel in the shape of a goose was left as a touching funerary offering in Gordion's Tumulus P, the grave of a royal child. In the same grave, dating from the late eighth century BC, lay the four-inch-long bronze quadriga, or chariot (left), with its team of four horses—probably a toy.

ferred that this was a waiting area, perhaps, for those seeking an audience with the officials who dwelled and worked inside. The seat, Young noticed, bore a number of drawings. Apparently scratched by Phrygians as they whiled away their time waiting, these and other graffiti showed boxers and warriors; lions, dogs, goats, and horses; and different types of birds. They also contained images of small houses with central doorways and gabled roofs that closely resembled the rock facade at Midas City described by Leake.

Subsequent excavations in the quarter unearthed more grandiose buildings—a dozen in all, the largest of which Young called the royal palace—grouped around two courtyards divided by a wall with a fine gateway. In this privileged enclave, the aristocrats of Gordion lived comparatively luxurious lives. The archaeologists found carved ivory plaques, inlays for long-disintegrated wooden furniture, and the remains of textiles—bits of felt, loosely woven hemp, and other fabrics—that Young guessed either hung on the walls or were draped on furniture. Decoratively stitched and fringed, the cloths must have created a pleasant setting for the eating and drinking that evidently took place there. Analysis of botanical remains has identified lentils, hazelnuts—probably from northern Anatolia—and to judge from 19 cherry pits recovered in the main room of the largest megaron, cornelian cherries among the foods consumed.

Evidently, the Phrygian well-to-do were in the habit of washing down such treats with beer. Like the Egyptians and Babylonians, they drank the beverage unfiltered—that is, with the barley husks still floating in it. They sipped the brew out of bowls using straws, or they poured it directly into their mouths from cleverly designed ceramic jugs. Six of these vessels turned up at Gordion, and others have been found in nearby tumuli. Each had a globular body, a single ear-shaped handle, and a projecting tubular spout, at the base of which was a small sieve for straining out the solids. Though the jugs were owned by the privileged few, this method of imbibing became so widely associated with the Phrygians in general that in the seventh century BC, the bawdy Greek poet Archilochos could be certain of drawing a laugh if he compared a certain sex act to a "Phrygian drinking his beer through a tube."

To the southeast of the large tumulus in Gordion's cemetery, Young and his team excavated a smaller burial belonging to a member of the Phrygians' privileged class. No trace remained of the skeleton other than the enamel of five teeth, from which an expert at the

URARTU, THE METALWORKING KINGDOM

On a rocky outcropping edged with medieval and Ottoman ruins *(above)* sit the cyclopean stone foundations of the citadel of Tushpa, the capital of Urartu, a kingdom renowned for its wealth and metalworking expertise. Dating from the mid-ninth century BC, the Urartian fortress strategically overlooked Lake Van in eastern Anatolia. The 11-inch-high bronze fragment *(inset)* suggests what the city may have looked like, with fortified walls and high towers.

The Urartians had reason to be on the defensive. They were engaged in continual warfare with the Assyrians, who sought control over the kingdom's mining areas. To this end Urartian metalworkers made bronze and iron armaments. As much artists as craftsmen, they also turned out an array of beautiful items. They outfitted chariot wheels, yokes, and harnesses with eye-catching bronze ornaments. And they decorated hammered bowls and cast cauldrons with images of deities and sacred animals.

The Urartians were tireless builders, using iron tools provided by the smiths to construct roads, forts, temples, and irrigation systems. But despite their military and economic prowess, they had succumbed to invaders from the north by 540 BC. While the Urartians would vanish, many of their metal products would survive, dispersed by trade and tribute to Phrygia, Greece, and Italy. In those places, as in Urartu, they would be dug up by archaeologists and offer proof of how gifted the Urartians were.

Similar to pectorals carved on Urartian bronze statuettes, the gold-plated silver pectoral at left corrals sacred lions, bulls, and winged creatures carrying ceremonial buckets. Below, an 8½-inch-high griffin was one of numerous cast-bronze mythical figures that decorated an elaborate throne.

A four-inch-high silver ceremonial bucket from Urartu demonstrates the skill of Urartian metalworkers. The delicate gold frieze shows a Sacred Tree ceremony, in which priestly figures hold buckets like this one as they anoint the tree, a religious act also depicted in Assyrian art.

One of a pair, this two-foot-high bronze, fan-shaped yoke standard decorated a Urartian chariot harness dating between the late ninth and early eighth century BC. Rendered in relief, a winged god stands on the back of a bull, holding pomegranate branches. He is supported by attending deities, who grip his outstretched wings.

This 3½-inch-high bronze bell, with windowed, octagonal sides, once graced a chariot harness. Urartian bronze objects were often inscribed with the name of the owner: The bell's inscription reads, "From the arsenal of Argishti," a king who reigned during the eighth century BC.

With pensive gaze, the profile of a young man reveals some of the masculine fashions of Lydia during the mid-fifth century BC—ringlets, earrings, white face, rouged cheeks, and a rouge-dotted nose and chin. Similar to Greek art of the period, the terra-cotta cup to which these two fragments belong may have been the work of a Greek potter residing in Anatolia or in a Greco-Anatolian setting.

University of Ankara deduced that the body had been that of a four- or five-year-old. The child had been laid to rest with nine beer jugs, which scholars speculate may or may not have been used for drinking beer. Also interred with the child were a mosaic-topped wooden table, a throne of boxwood inlaid with yew, and delicate wooden carvings of lions, a winged horse, and a yoked horned ox. The tomb's playful pottery—a pair of goose-shaped jugs that poured through the bill, and a ram-shaped vessel that poured from the mouth—evoked timeless children's pleasures, as did a small metal chariot, possibly a toy.

Only an industrious and orderly lower class could have supported such privilege, but what had its members left behind? Separated by a wall from the palace zone and raised on an artificial terrace to the west lay the remains of two rows of houses that contained evidence of the more mundane lives of the majority of Gordion's inhabitants. Two of the buildings lacked ovens or hearths and so would have been unlivable during Anatolia's frigid winters. These, Young surmised, must have served as storerooms. The others, however, appeared to be devoted to textile and food production. In them Young discovered the charred remains of wheat and barley and grinding stones for preparing flour. Kneeling in a row on a low brick platform, Phrygian slaves or, to judge from other ancient societies, the women of the various households rubbed boat-shaped stones over grain, while others mixed water with the resulting flour to make dough or placed the cakes into the ovens that also served to chase the chill from the air.

Along with clay cooking trays and iron tools, perhaps pokers for tending the fire, the archaeologists dug up many spindle whorls, an indication that thread was spun in the quarter, and large numbers of clay lumps pierced with holes. Called doughnuts by the excavators, these were loom weights. Fibers still clung to some, and the positioning of 21 others where they had fallen—in a straight line over five feet long—suggested that they had been dangling from the weaver's loom when the surprise attack came.

But such an appearance of domesticity cannot hide the fact that the Phrygians were a warlike people, led by Midas's imperial ambition into battles in the east described in the Assyrian palace records.

Indeed, a large combination ax and adze made of iron and found in the biggest megaron may have served as a Phrygian warrior's weapon of choice. Tiles from a building in the early-sixth-century-BC town of Pazarli, located 108 miles northeast of Ankara, give an idea of other equipment he and his colleagues may have carried to battle: The tiles' painted reliefs show a procession of men in plumed helmets carrying circular shields and small spears.

Since even aggressors must take defensive measures, the Phrygians of Midas City, Hattusha, and elsewhere surrounded their cities with stout walls and equipped them with subterranean passageways, staircases, shafts, and cisterns that would have been sources of water in case of siege. Gordion too was enclosed within defensive walls during the eighth century BC, but they failed to protect the city when the Cimmerian invaders arrived.

The destruction marked the end of Phrygian domination of Anatolia but by no means the end of habitation at Gordion. This Young would find out when he turned his attention to Küçük Höyük, or the "Little Mound," rising to the southeast of the main settlement, on the other side of a depression that he hazarded might mark the dried-up loop of the Sangarius River. There he discovered the remains of a Lydian settlement established in the century following the Cimmerian attack.

Mindful, perhaps, of what had transpired in the past, the Lydians had erected a 12-foot-thick crescent-shaped wall to protect their new town, as well as a three- or four-story building that might have sheltered a garrison. Yet even these precautions proved insufficient, as Küçük Höyük did not endure. Following an attack in the middle of the sixth century BC, the barracks were burned down, and soon after that, much of the settlement was buried beneath a large tumulus that had been built up over the body of a prominent warrior who fell in the battle.

The Lydians, of course, hailed from western Anatolia. For some 150 years, starting around 680 BC, they would control much of the previous Phrygian kingdom, including Gordion, while their capital at Sardis, standing near the Hermus River in the shadow of the steep Tmolus Mountains,

This 5½-inch-tall vase or ointment jar demonstrates a distinctive pottery form given the name lydion *because it originated in Lydia. Widely imitated in Greece and Etruria, such ceramic perfume vessels were decorated with thin paint brushed in broad, wavy strokes to imitate the appearance of glass or alabaster.*

95

emerged from the traditional Anatolian agrarian states and came into its own as an urban cultural center. Its influence would not only spread throughout the region but also prefigure the culture of classical Greece itself.

Economics drove the Lydian emergence. Commanding trade routes linking the plateau and the bustling Greek cities of the coast, Sardis was well positioned to benefit from growing commerce, and its citizens became rich trading goods such as pottery, some of which Young found at Kücük Höyük. A fertile river valley, forested mountain slopes, and an ample supply of minerals—gold in particular—no doubt enhanced Sardis's prosperity, prompting the snobbish Greek settlers along the coast to look down their noses at what they considered the excessive luxury of the Lydians. They complained of the Lydians' opulent living and "useless softnesses" and, in doing so, ensured that the name of the last Lydian ruler—Croesus—would survive in the expression "rich as Croesus."

Almost all archaeological investigations of the Lydians have concentrated on Sardis, site of excavations by a combined American team from the universities of Harvard and Cornell. Starting to dig there in 1958, the scientists had the pleasure of working in a landscape that is fertile and beautiful, planted as it is with orchards, vineyards, and fields of wheat, but they would become aware of some drawbacks as well. Heavy seasonal rains bring frequent floods, and the region is prone to seismic activity, which over the centuries has churned the site's occupation layers. "Lydian remains," the archaeologists wrote, "may be found deeply buried or close to the surface or even carried out of their original position by erosion, landslides, or earthquakes."

Nevertheless, excavations near a ford on the river Pactolus in what had been Sardis's market area have enabled the investigators to piece together a sequence of settlement stretching back to 1400 BC, and maybe even earlier. The first Lydian settlement emerged around 700 BC, at a time when the physical evidence at last started to jibe with written records, and especially with those left by Herodotus. He described the curious circumstances under which the dynasty that would rule Lydia during its 150-year flowering came to power. His tale begins around 685 BC, with the last king of the previous dynasty, Candaules, trying to convince the founder of the Mermnad line, his friend and minister Gyges, of the queen's unsurpassed loveliness: "Gyges, it is clear that you doubt what I tell you of my wife's beauty; seeing is believing, so we must contrive that you see her naked."

RECOVERING A STOLEN TREASURE

Holding tombs of sixth-century-BC Lydian rulers, the tumuli looming over farmlands in western Turkey had long been an inviting target for graverobbers. In the 1960s looters broke into three of them. Among the prizes they made off with were hundreds of silver and gold artifacts. To get at the treasures the thieves had to blow the top off one burial chamber with dynamite, and in another, they stripped the walls of frescoes, cutting them up to be sold separately.

The stolen items were bought by a dealer who slipped them out of the country with the help of the owner of a Turkish freight company. Later, one of the burglars, dissatisfied with his share, reported his fellow thieves to the police.

In 1970, Turkish authorities made several unsuccessful attempts to learn the details of a purchase of silver antiquities by New York's Metropolitan Museum of Art. That same year Turkish journalist Ozgen Acar, shown above *(at left)* with a participant in one robbery, committed himself to tracking down the so-called Lydian Hoard. At last in 1984, at a new Metropolitan exhibit of Greek and Roman artifacts, Acar recognized some of the stolen objects, having gotten descriptions of them from the apprehended looters.

It turned out that, in the 1960s, the museum had paid $1.7 million for 172 of the items. By the 1980s it owned about 250 pieces, valued in 1993 at $30 million. During a lawsuit brought by Turkey against the museum, the court was presented evidence worthy of a mystery novel. The thieves, in tearing out wall paintings, had left a fragment behind. A copy of it was shown to fit precisely into a fresco segment in the museum.

After losing the early rounds of litigation, the Metropolitan agreed to return the cache. Archaeologists see the case as a notable victory in the battle against art smuggling.

Inspired by an Egyptian symbol, this winged cloisonné sun disk has been fashioned as a pectoral. A carnelian glows at its center, and colored pastes contained by gold wires embellish the wings. Braided threads of gold form its chain and that of the bracelet (far left), which echoes the sun motif.

Acorn-shaped pendants, some with semiprecious stones, adorn the gold necklace on the right. The rings enclosed by the strand are set with multicolored agates. Below, a band of gold outlines each of two glass bracelets terminating in golden lion's-head finials.

The golden brooch above, about one inch wide and two inches high, represents a winged creature, half horse, half fish. Its scales, feathers, mane, and abstract design features stand out in detailed relief. Three sets of plaited gold tassels, terminating in glass beads, dangle from its body.

Gold reliefs decorate the silver bowl below. It corresponds to an almost-identical all-silver bowl from the sixth century BC that was found in Turkey. This match helped identify the artifact as Lydian, rather than East Greek, as it had been labeled in a Metropolitan Museum catalog.

One of the most highly prized of the recovered Lydian items is the silver wine pitcher above, known as an oinochoe. Its finely crafted handle is in the form of a naked youth grasping two lions by their tails. Two rams rest at the feet of the figure. Seven inches high, the vessel weighs 21 ounces.

Though Gyges objected, the king insisted that he hide behind the bedroom door and watch the queen preparing for bed, and the minister reluctantly agreed. The following morning, the queen called the official to her and, in the presence of the most trustworthy of her retinue, explained that she was aware of his cooperation with the king's plan. "You have seen me naked," she said. "You must therefore choose one of two courses. Either you must kill Candaules, marry me, and be king of Lydia, or you must perish here and now." Faced with such an unenviable choice, Gyges begged for forgiveness but found none to be received. Despairing, he finally opted to save himself and struck down the hapless king. News of the assassination spread quickly among the populace, who rebelled at the thought of being ruled by a murderer, and armed citizens took to the streets. Civil war was averted only at the eleventh hour, when Gyges received a blessing from the Greek oracle at Delphi, and order was restored.

The story is of genuine historical interest, for under Gyges the Lydians began a process of restless military expansion that would eventually leave them in control of much of the former Phrygian kingdom. The king's first targets, however, lay not to the east but to the west: the rich Greek coastal cities of Miletus, Smyrna, and Colophon. Pottery discovered at Sardis at the level where evidence of the first Lydian settlement turned up reflected a tradition of close relations with the Greeks, but now Gyges attacked his neighbors and sacked their cities, as his successors would later, probably in an effort to gain access to the Aegean Sea.

The discovery of traces of a conflagration at Sardis, the skeleton of a girl who had apparently been smothered in her sleep, and disarticulated bones bundled into an impromptu grave indicated that the Lydians were not always the aggressors, however. Like Gordion, Gyges' capital fell victim to the predations of nomadic hordes from north and east of the Black Sea who, the archaeologists think, were probably the Cimmerians. The fire dates to around the middle of the seventh century BC, and Assyrian annals confirm this date.

The scribes record that around 663 BC, Assyrian king Ashurbanipal received a messenger from Gyges requesting help in throwing back invaders. Yet the distance between the kingdoms was so great that Ashurbanipal had never heard of the Lydians or their language: "Of all the languages of East and of West, over which the god Ashur has given me control," he is quoted as saying, "there was no interpreter of his tongue. His language was foreign, so that his words

An early-fifth-century-BC Greek vase found in Etruria shows King Croesus about to be burned alive on a pyre. According to the historian Herodotus, Croesus invoked the Greek god Apollo to intercede, whereupon a thunderstorm put out the fire. Awestruck, the conquering Persian king Cyrus decided to spare Croesus.

100

were not understood." Still, some kind of aid may have been forthcoming: Gyges managed to repulse the attackers not once, but twice.

The ruler lost his life defending his clifftop citadel in 652 BC, but Lydian culture was to remain dynamic. In no time, the excavators found, the citizens of Sardis were again raising ambitious complexes as the town spread along the valley of the Pactolus. Indeed, all the signs pointed to a flowering urban society. The walls and floors, for example, were in better condition when excavated than those of Gyges' day, suggesting that the buildings were superior in construction.

Trade—indicated by the increasing number of imported Greek pots the diggers turned up—had flourished. Moreover, the pots were finer than earlier pieces; both ceramics from Corinth on the Greek mainland and locally made Lydian ware had grown lighter and less coarse, perhaps in order to satisfy the needs and tastes of an increasingly refined urban society. Prosperity spread from the city into the countryside; pollen studies suggest that farmers turned away from the livestock rearing on which the Lydians had depended to generate a greater variety of products, including oils and cereals.

The city's face changed with the lives of its inhabitants. At a level approximately corresponding to the period between 650 and 600 BC, the Harvard-Cornell team found traces of a walled business and industrial quarter—the Lydian Market. This, perhaps the forerunner of later bazaars, served as a focal point for the practice of crafts in which the Lydians were particularly skilled: pottery, leatherworking and metalsmithing, textile weaving and dyeing, cosmetics manufacture, ivory carving, gem cutting, and jewelry making.

The Lydians' greatest industry, however, evolved around gold. Indeed, Gyges and his successors would supply the majority of Greece's gold from around 650 to 550 BC, prompting classical authors such as Herodotus to refer to the river on which Sardis stood as the Golden Pactolus. The historian had ample reason to turn such a phrase, since he saw with his own eyes the 117 gold ingots—each about the size of a large encyclopedia volume—that Gyges donated to the sanctuary of Apollo at Delphi.

In 1960 the American excavators started work on what they called Pactolus North, where the crowded remains of buildings signaled a bustling sixth-century-BC Sardis suburb. Neighboring on a sacred enclosure lay two concentrations of small rings set in the ground. Numbering more than 100 and measuring as much as 11 inches across, the rings marked the sites of cupels, hollows that had been scooped out of the earth to be used as hearths, apparently for melting the gold dust from the Pactolus and other rivers. The process did not yield the metal in pure form, but as electrum, a naturally occurring silver-and-gold alloy. Electrum consisted of between 50 and 75 percent gold, an amount, incidentally, that was standard for the gold bullion and jewelry of the ancient Aegean world.

Herodotus claimed that the Lydians introduced the world's first coinage, originally of electrum, no doubt enhancing their status as traders. But modern analysis of the coins produced at the Sardis mint, stamped with the head of the imperial lion, shows that the gold content sometimes fell below 35 percent. So paltry an amount, some experts suggest, demonstrates that the Lydian rulers may have been cheating their merchants by adding silver to the coins. If this is so, the deceit became known and the electrum currency quickly lost the confidence of the traders on whom the Lydian economy depended.

Fortunately, the Lydians were able to restore credibility under Croesus, who introduced coins of pure gold or silver. They accomplished this, the excavators of Pactolus North learned, by means of a simple and ingenious technique. They hammered the electrum into sheets and then placed it in pots between layers of crushed brick and salt. These they heated for several days in furnaces. As the process went forward, the silver in the electrum combined with the salt, leaving behind pure gold.

The new coinage no doubt served to improve the Lydians' trade contacts with their Greek neighbors. Yet, as shown by excavators at Bayrakli, a northern district of the modern city of Izmir, the successors of Gyges still looked greedily toward the rich Greek cities of the Ionian coast. Working in the northwest corner of the site, the

The sixth-century-BC gold coin at top and the silver one below it from Sardis, the capital of Lydia, are imprinted with heads of a lion and bull, insignias of royal power. Both pieces may have been struck during the reign of King Croesus, when gold coins were known to have been used for money, or during the Persian occupation of Lydia. The Lydians are credited with minting the first coins.

location of the ancient city of Smyrna, the archaeologists explored a mound 65 feet high that had once been a siege ramp. Piled up by attackers to breach the city walls, it must have offered commanding fields of fire to the Lydian archers and slingers who made it to the top. Arrowheads littered the site, some still embedded in the mud-brick walls of the city's houses. Studying sherds from the mound, the excavators placed the assault around 600 BC, a date fitting well with the historical record of an attack by one of Gyges' successors, Alyattes, who reigned from about 610 to 560 BC.

Alyattes was credited with finally driving the Cimmerians from Anatolia and bringing the old Phrygian kingdom under increasing Lydian control. But eastward expansion made Alyattes clash with the Medes, who with the Babylonians had brought an end to the Assyrian empire. For five years, the two sides fought sporadically. Then, in 585 BC—the year can be dated exactly thanks to a solar eclipse that, according to Herodotus, occurred during the final battle—the enemies agreed on a border, the Halys River, and made peace. The kings sealed the agreement with a marriage between their offspring.

After the war, Alyattes turned his attention to the construction of a suitable memorial, a tomb that would ultimately rival Midas's tumulus at Gordion. The Lydian aristocracy buried their dead in a vast cemetery located about six miles north of Sardis on a limestone ridge between the Hermus River and the Gygean Lake. Called Bin Tepe, or "1,000 mounds," in Turkish, the cemetery in fact contains more than 100 large graves, the most imposing of which are known as the Royal Mounds and date back to the reign of Gyges. In 1962 the Harvard-Cornell team made a careful plan of the biggest in the area, Alyattes' grave, but chose not to excavate, since 19th-century investigators had already determined that the mound had been plundered, probably in Roman times. Of the five markers that Herodotus described as standing atop the barrow, only one remained, a budlike block of stone.

Classical sources identified another mound, standing about 170 feet high and more than 650 feet wide just over a mile south of the Gygean Lake on a limestone ridge, as that of Gyges. Applying electrical resistivity techniques, the excavators distinguished the ancient base of the mound from the thick layer of earth that centuries of erosion had washed down from the tumulus; and using an oil-

drilling rig borrowed from the excavators at Gordion, they tried without success to locate the tomb. Finally, they tunneled into it but found only the rubbish of ancient graverobbers. On the way, they encountered a wall of limestone blocks that might have marked the original circumference of the tumulus, 295 feet in diameter. Engraved on the stones were several enigmatic marks, the meaning of which remains puzzling today: One interpretation is that they read "GuGu," the Assyrian name for Gyges; another claims that they are little more than masons' marks giving instructions to the builders.

Regardless of whether the tumulus was once the resting place of the founder of the Mermnad dynasty, the vast effort required to raise such an awesome monument shows the degree to which the Lydians were prepared to commemorate their dead. And although by no means all citizens received such splendid memorials—others were buried in rock-cut tombs, cist graves made of stone slabs, or terra-cotta sarcophagi—the elite at least were laid to rest with gold, silver, and fine garments. Inscriptions placed in the graves put them under divine protection against tomb robbers.

The wealth evidenced in the finest Lydian burials had reached its peak during the reign of Croesus, who ascended the throne of his

A young warrior found at Sardis still clasps in his bony hand a stone, a missile that he was ready to throw moments before his death. Physical anthropologists determined that he fell or was thrown from a height, dying in violent circumstances, possibly of a wound inflicted from behind during the capture of the capital by the Persian army about 546 BC. Lying anonymously in the debris of the city's destroyed fortifications, the skeleton cannot be identified as either Lydian or Persian.

Less than 20 feet from the warrior's skeleton, archaeologists found fragments of a bronze-decorated iron helmet (top). *A modern steel-and-bronze reconstruction* (above) *by the Royal Armouries in London, was assembled from eight wedge-shaped plates, arranged radially. Decorative cords accent the seams between the plates, and the cheek guards are hinged. The helmet is either Lydian or Persian.*

father, Alyattes, in 560 BC. Establishing friendly relations with the Greek ports on the Ionian coast, Croesus greatly expanded the commercial opportunities for his merchants and showed his thanks by presenting rich treasures of gold and silver to various Greek temples. To Greek historians it seemed that Croesus lived in much the same way as an Ionian Greek, only on a far more splendid scale.

But the seeds of Croesus's fall were already sown. A new power was rising in the east, where the Persian Cyrus had overthrown the Medes to establish what would become the Achaemenid dynasty. Croesus, wrongly sensing that his new adversary was weak, decided to break Alyattes' treaty with the Medes and seize the rich provinces across the Halys River. Emboldened by an oracle from the sanctuary of Apollo at Delphi, who predicted—ambiguously—that Croesus would destroy a mighty empire if he went to war against the Persians, the king moved eastward. But unfortunately for him, the realm that would ultimately go down was his own.

After an inconclusive battle east of the Halys, Croesus returned to Sardis for the winter and sent home those of his troops who were not Lydians. Cyrus, however, chose to disregard the end of the traditional campaigning season and followed his adversary back to the Hermus plain. Understrength and completely surprised, the Lydian rallied his renowned horsemen to mount a last-minute counterattack, but the ensuing battle went to the Persians, for Cyrus came up with a clever way to blunt the assault: According to Herodotus, he ordered a train of baggage camels moved to his front line, where the smell of the beasts so upset the Lydian horses that the cavalry charge ended in chaos, and the way to the capital lay open.

But Sardis's 65-foot-thick stone and mud-brick walls were probably not breached without a bitter struggle. Excavating in their rubble in 1988, the American archaeologist Crawford H. Greenewalt Jr. uncovered the skeleton of a male whom a physical anthropologist identified as being between the ages of 22 and 26. Apparently a warrior, he must have died during the hand-to-hand fighting that culminated in the collapse of the defenses, for the bones of his left forearm had been broken in two places, as if he had tried to defend himself against a sword-wielding attacker. In his right hand he still clutched a stone the size of an apricot. Struck down from behind during the desperate fight, he breathed his last before he could loose his missile. Nearby lay the badly corroded remains of a helmet that may have belonged either to a Lydian or to one of his Persian enemies.

Herodotus relates that Croesus retired to the citadel high above the city while the battle raged, and for a while the bastion appeared impregnable, but luck was with Cyrus. After a fortnight's siege, one of the attackers watched a Lydian soldier scramble down the hill in pursuit of his helmet, which he had dropped, and thus discovered a hidden path to the summit. Climbing up the sheer cliffs by the same route the next day, the Persians took the remaining defenders by surprise and stormed the acropolis.

Croesus was taken prisoner and sentenced to die, but his fate is unclear, since his figure passed into myth among the Greeks—and became a popular subject for Greek vase painters *(page 101)*—almost immediately after his death. The artists and storytellers were no doubt enamored of Croesus's wealth and of his dramatic reversal of fortune, which to Greek eyes seemed fitting atonement for the sins of his ancestor, Gyges the usurper. But hubris may also have played a role in guaranteeing his lasting fame.

Years before the Persian debacle, Herodotus wrote, Croesus received an esteemed visitor from Athens: the well-known legislator and statesman Solon. Croesus at the time was enjoying life at the pinnacle of his power and prosperity and was eager to have his status acknowledged by one of the most famous Greeks of the age. So he is said to have asked his guest a leading question: "Whom would you consider to be the happiest of men?" Mindful of what the king wanted to hear but unimpressed by the trappings of luxury, Solon uttered what must have been an unpalatable reply: "No man," he observed, "can be deemed happy until the manner of his death is known."

That the Lydian kingdom fell to the Persians no doubt made the story all the more poignant to Herodotus's readers, who may have found fault in Croesus's excessive pride but still admired his brave stand against a people the Greeks would come to regard as only somewhat more than barbarians. Indeed, in later generations—while the remains of the great cultures of Anatolia disappeared under new settlements and the peninsula increasingly took on the role of bridge between the great civilizations of east and west—it would be the mainland Greeks who crossed swords with the descendants of Cyrus in a huge and bloody struggle for dominance in the ancient world.

SOMETHING WORTH SEEING

In 1957, when University of Pennsylvania excavation director Rodney Young cut through the wooden wall of the tomb chamber beneath the largest tumulus at Gordion, thought to be the burial place of King Midas, he exposed treasures unseen for 2,700 years. Young found no gold, silver, or jewels there. But rarer and more valuable by far was the wooden furniture that lay scattered about in various states of disrepair—15 pieces in all, displaying unparalleled intricacy of design, exquisite craftsmanship, and powerful religious symbolism *(above)*.

Because so few pieces of wooden furniture have survived from the past, archaeologists' knowledge of ancient woodworking was previously based primarily on articles retrieved from tombs, such as those of King Tutankhamen and Bronze Age Jericho, and on whatever could be gleaned from wall paintings and written accounts.

In the fifth century BC, the Greek historian Herodotus spoke of a throne given to the Sanctuary of Apollo at Delphi by King Midas of Phrygia, the first non-Greek to make an offering there. Herodotus wrote that the throne was "well worth seeing," and though no descriptions or remnants of the throne survive, the discovery of the extraordinary furniture at Gordion provides clues to its beauty. More important, the furniture has much to say about the people who made it. "It is the finds at Gordion that best illuminate the Phrygians, their tastes, and their special artistic temperament," says the archaeologist Elizabeth Simpson, director of the Gordion Furniture Project. Together with senior conservator Krysia Spirydowicz and a team of experts, Simpson has spent 15 years restoring the magnificent pieces.

THE ROYAL BURIAL CHAMBER

As Young and his team peered through the hole cut in the wooden tomb wall, they found themselves poised over the skeleton itself, seen at right in a photograph taken shortly after they entered the tomb. (The three pillars were erected by the archaeologists to keep the log ceiling from collapsing.)

At first Young interpreted the funeral bier as a four-poster bed. However, subsequent study of the fragments by Simpson revealed that the king had actually been buried in a coffin made from an enormous log. As the drawing below shows, it had removable side rails, with four wooden blocks that braced the rounded coffin body. In order to lower the heavy coffin into the tomb, ropes may have been passed under the ledges at both ends and through grooves cut in their sides.

Showing the ravages of time, the wooden ledge at the head of the log coffin (above) lies where it broke off sometime after the king's burial in the eighth century BC. A three-legged wooden table next to it had collapsed, spilling a bag of bronze fibulae—ancient safety pins. More than 180 fibulae lay scattered around the skeleton and on the floor.

The king's wooden coffin (below) measured more than 10 feet long and 3 feet wide. It was produced by cutting a section of a huge cedar tree in two lengthwise and hollowing out one half.

Seen as they were found, two of three massive bronze cauldrons sit in iron ring stands against the south wall. Bronze bowls and collapsed wooden tables lie strewn across the floor. The presence of the cauldrons, bowls, and tables, along with two serving stands, bronze pitchers, and ladles, suggests that a funeral banquet had been held and that the furnishings were interred with the king.

The plan below of the burial chamber shows the location of the skeleton and coffin in the northwest corner, as well as the placement of the many grave goods, including 170 bronze vessels. The 21-by-17-foot room had no windows or doors, indicating that the coffin, the furniture, and other contents had been lowered into the chamber from above.

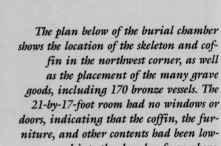

A masterpiece of metalworking, this bronze bucket was produced in the shape of a ram's head; another took the form of a lion's head. The vessels had been wrapped in cloth that disintegrated over time, with only tatters of fabric remaining. Both animal buckets, with their realistic-looking inlaid eyes, may have been intended as offerings to the deceased.

The hammered bronze ladle at left is one of two found on the floor near two wooden serving stands. The bronze omphalos bowl above, sculpted with petal-shaped relief, was among the 100 bowls recovered. Many of these had been stacked on eight wooden tables. The 20-inch-high bronze cauldron below, decorated with cast-bronze winged deities, probably held food or drink.

MIRACLES OF PHRYGIAN ARTISTRY

Remarkably preserved, one of the inlaid serving stands leans against the *wall of the tomb. A bronze, petaled omphalos bowl sits upright in front of it.*

Due in part to the low humidity that prevailed inside the sealed chamber, 15 pieces of Phrygian furniture survived their two millennia of entombment, some in better condition than others. In addition to the massive log coffin, these consisted of three badly deteriorated wooden stools, eight three-legged plain tables, one elaborately carved and inlaid table, and two standing pieces, which Young initially thought were throne backs or screens.

After careful study, extensive conservation by Simpson and her team, and meticulous reassembly of the fragments, these so-called throne backs or screens proved to be ornately inlaid serving stands. The inlaid faces with their intricate patterns had been skillfully assembled by mortise-and-tenon joinery. The woodworkers, however, had done more than simply exercise their craft: As Simpson would discover, they had incorporated into the patterns symbols and motifs that held special meaning for the Phrygians.

Simpson fills in a portion of a serving stand's decayed walnut leg with Plexiglas. Because the stands were *too delicate to bear their own weight, Plexiglas mounts supported on metal stands were made to hold them upright.*

One of the two 37-inch-high serving stands displays the intricate design that covers the inlaid boxwood face. A rosette medallion supported by twin curving forms interrupts the orderly geometry. The carvers executed the inlay by inscribing patterns in the boxwood with a sharply pointed tool, then chiseling out channels and recesses for darker, juniper-wood inlays, which they tapped into place, and finally finishing the surface.

As seen from behind in the archaeologist's drawing at right, the serving stand has a single back leg, with four angled boxwood struts to support a carved walnut shelf. Three circular openings in the top held small bronze cauldrons from which food or drink may have been ladled during the banquet.

A SUBTLE INTERPLAY OF SYMBOLS

The decorative beauty of the serving stands may have been more than pleasing to the Phrygian eye—indeed, according to Simpson, the objects may have held religious meaning. She hypothesizes that their design replicates sacred shrines like the eighth-century-BC Midas Monument at left, dedicated to the Phrygian mother goddess Kybele. Analyzing such stone structures, Simpson takes note of their characteristics: a facade covered with geometric, maze-like patterns and a central niche that might hold a statue of the goddess. Simpson observes that the stands reflect both the shrines' shape and geometric decoration. Further, she suggests that the central rosette may symbolize the deity, just as a star rosette in Assyrian art signifies the goddess Ishtar. The two curving portions leading from the rosette down to the feet may be abstract lion's legs, representing the lions that sometimes are depicted as attending Kybele.

The 52-foot-high facade of the Midas Monument in the Phrygian highlands (left, above) was carved into a cliff. The central niche probably held a statue of the goddess Kybele resembling the much-eroded one at left from a similar shrine at Arslan Kaya, also in the highlands. Here the goddess is depicted with two lions that stand to either side, touching her head with their paws.

Even on the slightly damaged pieces of the serving stand above, seen here after conservation and cleaning, regular rows of squares set within an inlaid-lattice background give an impression of harmony and balance. Seemingly alike, on closer examination the squares turn out to be varied, lending the apparently symmetrical design a hidden dynamic.

Shown below is a meander square, one of the two types of designs used by the woodworkers in the 192 squares covering the face of the serving stand seen at left. By subtly manipulating the bars and hooks of such squares, the artisans introduced variations that added interest to the puzzlelike sequences.

As part of the stand's overall richness, two types of inlaid designs were disposed in alternating rows, as diagrammed at right, with yellow representing meander squares and blue swastikalike shapes. For variety, the woodworkers played with the two types of designs: In addition to using two basic designs, they also rotated them 90 degrees and flopped them.

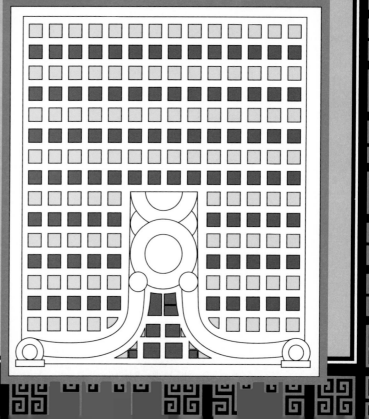

A TABLE PIECED BACK TOGETHER

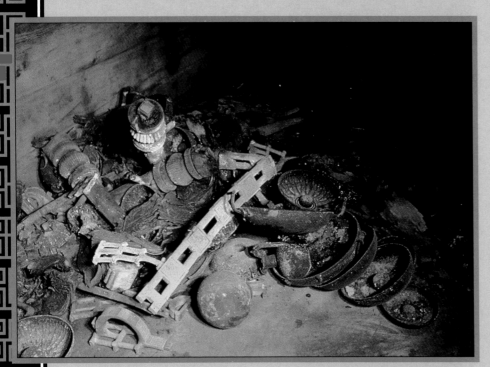

As first seen by the excavators in 1957, the inlaid table had collapsed, spilling its load of bronze vessels to the floor. But the table had fallen in such a way that its square form could eventually be determined.

Simpson and Turkish conservator Nazif Uygur inject a bonding agent between pieces of a Plexiglas frame built to support the fragile table. Eighteen vertical struts like those seen here run around its upper portion.

A tribute to modern restorers' skills as well as to the artistry of the ancient Phrygian wood-workers, the inlaid table—whimsically named the Pagoda Table by Young because aspects of it reminded him of Asian pagodas—required more than five years of patient work to research, conserve, and reassemble. The initial treatment of the table produced shrinkage and discoloration, and the wood had to be conserved again before the pieces could be reassembled.

The table was constructed from 40 major parts, all expertly fitted together with mortise-and-tenon joinery. The wood of the frame and legs is boxwood and the inlay juniper; the now-disintegrated top was walnut. The three-legged table has four handles, a sign that it probably functioned as a portable banquet table. The three legs ensured its stability on uneven flooring.

Like the serving stands, the table shows the Phrygian love of intricacy: It is inlaid with rosette-like designs placed next to recti-linear and mazelike ones. To Simpson, the patterns' order and variety propose and then defy symmetry—a game that she believes must have been intentional. By playing with the designs, the Phrygians added surprises and limited repetition. All this adds up to a lively, provocative work of art.

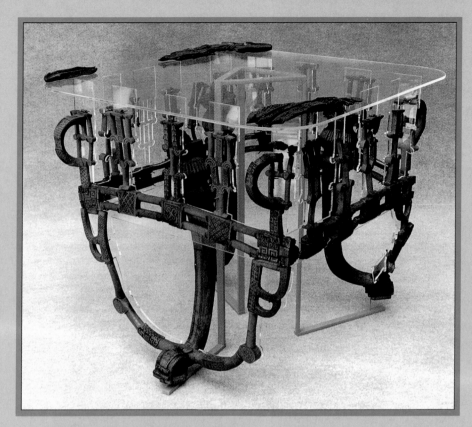

Fully restored, the inlaid table is mounted for display in the Museum of Anatolian Civilizations in Ankara, with a Plexiglas top that supports the few remnants of the original walnut surface, much of which had crumbled to dust. The table is 25 inches high and 31 inches wide.

Simpson's drawing of the three-legged inlaid table shows how the piece looked when new. It reveals the intricacy of the design and the vitality of its maker's imagination. The front leg is braced by a curving strut that seems to lift the table's frame off the ground. The interplay of the carved shapes and inlaid patterns adds to the compelling nature of this masterpiece.

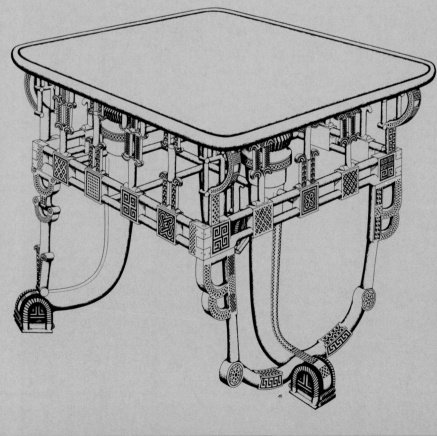

The ornate leg strut above twists markedly to join the abstracted claw foot of the left rear leg. Rows of delicate juniper diamonds and triangles like the ones visible here create varied patterns on each leg strut.

THE OTHER GREECE—PROUD LAND OF THE PIONEERS

Hybrid in design, this 15-inch-tall wine pitcher made in about 635 BC illustrates the combining of cultures that occurred in the Ionic cities of Anatolia. The shape comes from the Greek mainland, but the decorative style is eastern.

Two-thirds of the way down the west coast of Turkey, facing the Greek island of Samos, stands a mountain known from ancient times as Mycale, the scene of a famous Greek victory over the Persians in 479 BC. In its shadow lies a smaller hill, called *Otomatik Tepe,* or "Automatic Hill," from its more recent use as a machine-gun post, notably during the First World War and the following Greco-Turkish War. Here in 1957 German archaeologists succeeded in locating a once-important ancient site—the Panionium, where more than 2,500 years ago representatives of the Panionian League of Greek settlers in Anatolia held their religious assembly, discussed matters of common concern, and celebrated a great festival in honor of Poseidon, the god of the sea and of earthquakes.

The excavators found traces of the council chamber, lined on three sides by stepped rows of seats, where delegates from the 12 cities that made up the league gathered for deliberations. The few courses of gray stonework were physically unspectacular. Yet they had a special historical resonance, for the complex was the nearest that the Greeks who colonized the western coast of Anatolia ever came to creating a single political center, and its stones echoed to speeches described in the writings of the classical historians.

The first to arrive, the Ionians constituted only one part of the great surge of Greek settlement that transformed western Anatolia around 1000 BC and in the following years. Two other waves of colonists—the Aeolians and later the Dorians—also crossed the Aegean at this time, driven by unsettled conditions in their European homeland. Each group came from a separate part of Greece, and after arriving in Asia Minor, each retained a distinctive identity; even the accents of their members were markedly different.

Between them, the three groups were to make a contribution to the heritage of the world out of all proportion to their relatively small numbers—and they would do so long before the person commonly associated with the spread of Hellenism, Alexander the Great, arrived on the scene. The father of Greek poetry, Homer, counted among their ranks, as did many of the early philosophers. Important schools of sculpture and vase painting flourished in the new environment, and in architecture the Anatolian Greeks contributed the free-flowing Ionic style. Indeed, the scale and magnificence of the buildings with which they adorned their beautiful marble cities amazed ancient visitors. Two such edifices—the Mausoleum of Halicarnassus and the Temple of Artemis (or, as the Romans called her, Diana) at Ephesus—ranked among the Seven Wonders of the World.

The East Greeks, as they are now known, were also great seafarers and explorers. Their merchants crisscrossed the Mediterranean, carrying cargoes of sponges, luxury goods, pottery, and wine, and some even sailed through the Strait of Gibraltar to do business with traders inhabiting what is now Spain's Atlantic coast. In time the Anatolian Greeks sent out colonists of their own. They were mariners from tiny Phocaea, about 20 miles northwest of Smyrna, who first explored the western Mediterranean and who settled what was to become Marseilles. Other adventurers passed through the Bosporus to scout the resources of the Black Sea region, and the stories they brought back of its riches gave rise to the legend of Jason and the Golden Fleece. By 700 BC, settlers inspired by such tales followed the explorers, and it was through their efforts that centers of Greek civilization eventually ringed the body of water that in earlier times had been known, for its rough conditions, as the Inhospitable Sea.

Alongside the Hellenes lived the Mysians, Carians, Lydians, and Lycians, native populations who were either indigenous to Anatolia or who had migrated there earlier. Each occupied its own defined territory, coexisting for the most part peacefully with the newcomers. Some, like the Carians, mixed freely with the Greeks. The Lycians, however, kept aloof and fiercely guarded their independence. But even they were not immune to the attractions of Greek civilization—the alphabet and, foremost, the political entity known as a polis, or city-state. Indeed, Hellenism ultimately extended its influence not just along the western edges of the Aegean and Mediterranean Seas but also across Anatolia and beyond.

In many ways nature favored the coast to which the colonists came more than the regions they left behind. The winters were milder than in many parts of the homeland, and the soil, watered by seasonal rains, was more fertile. Orchards, olive groves, and vineyards flourished on it, and forest-clad hills nearby provided materials for building ships and houses.

Other aspects of the geographical situation were less helpful, at least to the development of a unified state. The coastal strip was narrow and deeply indented, and only the four great valleys of the Caicus, Hermus, Cayster, and Maeander Rivers in the central part provided access through the mountainous hinterland to the Anatolian interior. Bays and mountain spurs separated many of the seaside settlements from their neighbors, directing the newcomers' gaze toward the water's horizon rather than inward to the continent of Asia. The self-contained communities that developed had little inclination to band together into larger political groupings, jealous as they were of their own cultural identities, and they were easily picked off by stronger rivals and invaders.

As a result, the Greek Anatolian cities eventually fell under the sway of a succession of foreign rulers, the first of which were the Lydian kings, who began their raids in the seventh century BC. When the Persian conqueror Cyrus the Great defeated and captured Croesus, the last of the Lydian monarchs, in 546 BC, the cities the Lydians had annexed were added to the Achaemenid empire, as were the rest of Croesus's dominions. His capital at Sardis became the headquarters of Persian rule in western Anatolia.

In the wake of Xerxes' disastrous invasion of mainland Greece and the Persian defeats at Salamis in 480 BC and Plataea the following year, the cities of the Anatolian coast nominally regained independence, but in practice they came under the sway of Athens, the dominant force in the victorious Greek alliance. The Athenians proved in time to be as interfering and as onerous in their demands as the former imperial masters, and for the most part the Anatolian

Greeks were happy enough to slip back into the Persian sphere of influence. They remained there for much of the fourth century BC, until the meteoric irruption of Alexander the Great brought the power of Persia's Achaemenid rulers to an end.

The Macedonian conqueror's sudden death in 323 BC in Babylon heralded the dawn of a confused age: Rival contenders struggled for supremacy over the far-flung territories that he had ruled, and fortunes and allegiances changed rapidly. In time, local dynasts in the Anatolian city of Pergamon were able to build up a mini-empire of their own, controlling much of the Aegean coast. But by the second century BC, a new imperial power—Rome—was on the horizon. When the last Greek ruler of Pergamon bequeathed his realm in his will to the Roman imperium in 133 BC, he in effect settled the fate of much of the coastal lands for the next 500 years.

The Greeks had so long been present in Anatolia that the story of their development can hardly be separated from that of the emergence of Greece itself. It began almost a millennium before the power shift at Pergamon, with the appearance of the first settlers sometime during the dark period following the collapse of the great Bronze Age civilization of Mycenaean Greece in the 13th or 12th centuries BC. The question of when the settlers arrived is a vexed one. Signs of them in the archaeological record come in the form of pottery in a style known as protogeometric, originating from Athens. Excavators have turned up sherds of the ware at half a dozen sites in Ionia and have dated most to the 10th century BC. It seems likely, then, that the initial wave of migration was already rolling by 1000 BC, when Athens was still nothing more than a village.

Evidence of earlier contacts between the eastern Aegean and the civilizations of Mycenae and Minoan Crete has complicated the situation. Mycenaean pottery has been found on several of the Greek islands off the Anatolian coast and at such mainland sites as Ephesus, Colophon, and Miletus. Archaeologists have also found a substantial walled settlement that stood at Miletus during the Late Bronze Age, leading some historians to speculate that the city might have been the Millawanda referred to in 15th-century-BC Hittite texts. According to the documents, Millawanda was where the representative of the great king of an otherwise unidentified power known as Ahhiyawa lived. Ahhiyawa apparently lay overseas and, according to some scholars, might have been the Achaean kingdom of Mycenae.

The early pottery record at Miletus in fact shows contact with

WHAT A WONDER LOOKED LIKE

The Greek poet Antipater made no bones about his favorite among the Seven Wonders of the World: In his view, the Temple of Artemis at Ephesus put the six others "in the shade." But when he wrote this, around 130 BC, the temple, or Artemision, still existed. By the time the 18th-century Austrian architect Johann Fischer von Erlach produced his re-creation *(right, below)*, complete with a four-column porch, he had to base it on written sources and ancient coins showing the structure.

Now, thanks to years of excavation, archaeologists have a bit more to go on. The surviving foundation—originally 255 feet wide and 425 feet long—shows that the front of the temple sported eight columns, on which a huge pediment rested. Sculpted column drums recovered at the site, like the one at far right, suggest that these were decorated. But were the friezes located at the top or bottom of the columns? One modern German archaeologist's drawing *(background)* positions them at eye level, but until further evidence turns up, the question must remain open.

122

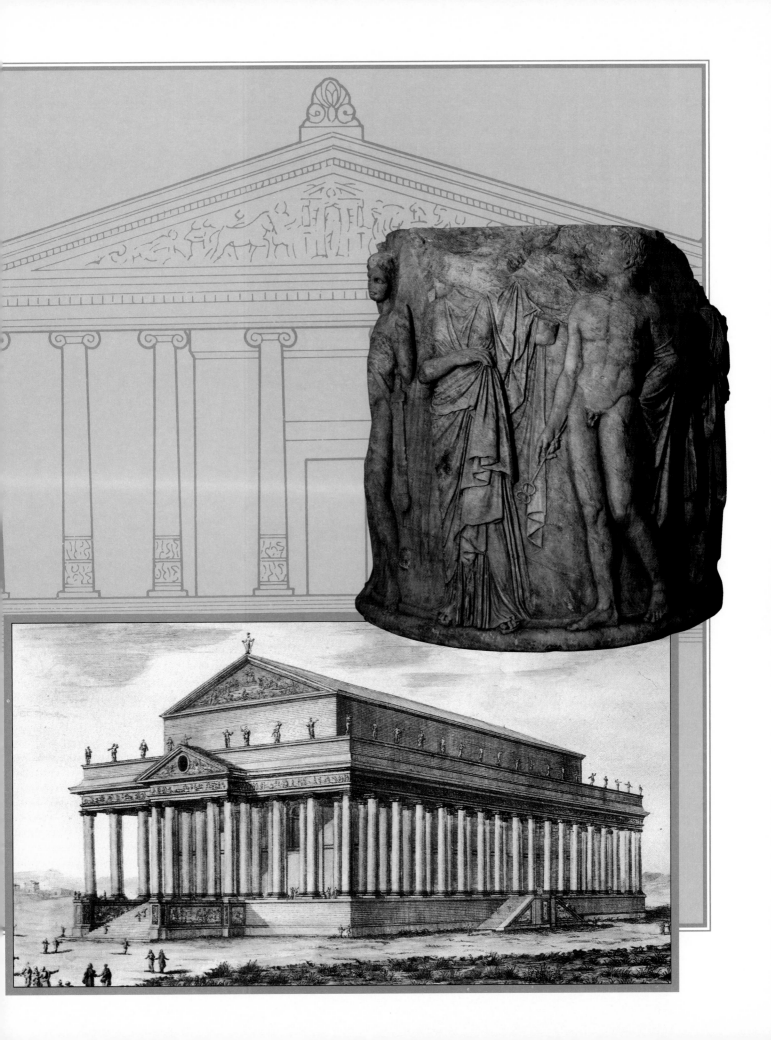

Minoan Crete as well as Mycenae from as early as the 15th century BC. The settlement seems to have survived the demise of the mainland Mycenaean centers, only to be destroyed sometime in the following century. Homer mentions Miletus in the *Iliad,* but as a Carian city. Herodotus too claims that the first Ionian settlers found the location occupied by Carians. He goes on to report that the pioneers, having brought no womenfolk with them, slaughtered the local men and took their women for wives. The massacre, he wrote, explained a longstanding refusal on the part of the women of Miletus either to dine with their husbands or to address them by name.

The balance of the evidence, then, suggests that there was a mysterious break in Greek occupation of the site, and little supports the theory, floated by some historians, that the first wave of immigrants may have been sent to Asia Minor to bolster existing Greek settlements. It is possible, though, that the colonists drew on lingering memories of earlier contacts with the inhabitants of the area, and scholars are certain that the newcomers were familiar with the Anatolian coastline, perhaps through trade and fishing.

As classical historians told it, the Aeolians, a people from Thessaly and Boeotia in mainland Greece, made up the first of the three waves of colonists. Even centuries afterward, visitors claimed to hear in the descendants' speech a similarity to the dialect spoken in the homeland. The initial Aeolian settlements were clustered on the island of Lesbos, 15 miles offshore, which served as their base. Its principal city, Mytilene, was to remain an important Aeolian center throughout the classical and later periods.

Mysians occupied the area just east of the island. A feisty native people, they firmly resisted incursions into their lands and provided an effective obstacle to expansion for the newcomers. When the Aeolians eventually spread out, they moved southeast, where they established Pitane and Cyme, and to the north, where they settled a region stretching from their mountaintop city of Assos, ringed by almost three miles of stone walls, to the Dardanelles. Here immigrants revived Troy, which had been destroyed and abandoned at a time later identified with the disaster of Homer's Trojan War.

The Aeolians were to be quickly overshadowed by the Ionians who settled the coast farther south. With the exception of Lesbos and some of its settlements, most of the northern colonists were conservative in temper, averse to confrontation, and largely agricultural in their interests. Until the fifth century BC, when Mytilene surrendered to Athens, they showed little of the commercial or intellectual flair of their southern cousins. They apparently submitted without resistance to the Lydians, the Persians, and Alexander in turn, before eventually being subsumed into the kingdom of Pergamon and thence into the Roman province of Asia.

The Ionians proved to be an altogether more cantankerous bunch. According to later writers such as the Greek geographers Strabo and Pausanias, they were refugees from the northern Peloponnese who first found their way to Athens and then sailed eastward—or so the stories would have it—in groups led by various sons of a legendary ruler of Athens, King Codrus. Codrus himself may never have existed, but scholars have assembled good historical evidence of the Athenian connection, in the form of shared festivals and cults as well as a similar calendar. The Ionians so valued their relationship with Athens that those among them able to trace their lineage back to it enjoyed special status. According to Herodotus, those Greeks whose ancestors started for Anatolia from Government House in Athens considered themselves the purest Ionians.

The pioneers were lucky to have come ashore in the middle reaches of Anatolia's west coast. Herodotus explains they "had the good fortune to establish their settlements in a region that enjoys a better climate than any other we know of. It does not resemble what is found either farther north, where there is an excess of cold and wet, or farther south, where the weather is both too hot and too dry."

One feature of the coastal landscape, however, was to have a profound and damaging long-term impact on many of the settlements, most of which grew up around the mouths of seasonal mountain torrents. Often, as the rivers flowed down from the heights where they had their source, they brought huge amounts of mud, which they deposited at the shore, creating vast mud flats. The spreading silt gradually cut off cities that depended on the sea for their livelihood, and in some cases the muck threatened to engulf them altogether. As a result, many of the once-great ports now lie well inland. Ephesus is today half a dozen miles from the Aegean, while visitors to Miletus have to climb one of the local hills to catch a glimpse of the sea.

The early communities were generally set defensively on the ends of peninsulas or on offshore islands, perched precariously on the outermost tip of what the newcomers obviously regarded as a continent inhabited by hostile peoples. As it turned out, they met less resistance than they had feared. In fact, the coast appears to have been underpopulated, and the indigenous populations that the Greeks encountered were insufficiently organized to pose much of a threat.

Although the literary sources mention many names, by far the most significant of the Anatolian groups were the Carians, whose heartland in historical times lay to the south of the Ionian lands and stretched from Miletus on the Aegean to the border of Lycia on the Mediterranean. The Greeks believed that the Carians once lived on islands and manned the ships of Minos, the king of Crete. And there is no doubt that the Carians were mariners, famous as sailors and mercenaries, even pirates. Some scholars assume that they descended from a Late Bronze Age people called the Karkisa, who are reported to have fought with the Hittites against the pharaoh Ramses II at the Battle of Kadesh. Archaeological evidence in the form of potsherds suggests that they also were in close contact with both Minoan Crete and Mycenaean Greece. Homer speaks of Carians "barbarous of speech" in the *Iliad* and lists them among the allies of the Trojans.

The Carians who lived inland in villages and in a few towns practiced agriculture and some became prominent landowners. They were also capable soldiers whom Herodotus credited with being the inspiration for the Greeks' subsequent use of crests on helmets and of devices and handles on shields, which had previously gone undecorated and were worn slung over the shoulder. In later years the Carians won a reputation as effective mercenaries. In fact, much of what little is known of their language comes from graffiti that Carian and Ionian soldiers carved on the legs of the colossal statues at Abu Simbel in Egypt early in the sixth century BC, when they were accompanying the pharaoh Psammetichos on an expedition into Nubia.

Although the Carians used their military skills to protect their heartland, they apparently were not present in sufficient numbers on the Ionian coast to challenge the Greek immigrants seriously. The settlements prospered, and the towns began to spread. Some island sites were abandoned, and the major Ionian communities expanded inland—though rarely by more than 20 to 30 miles—to create the self-sufficient city-states that were standard for all Greek colonies.

Farther south, the only substantial Greek presence came from

A GREEK CITY THAT GOT LEFT BEHIND

After Priene had existed for some 600 years on a bank of the winding Maeander River (from which the word *meander* comes), Ionian city fathers of the fourth century BC were obliged to move the town away from the flood plain. Ever-mounting deposits of river-borne silt had made the site impractical. The new Priene was to be built several hundred feet above the old city on a narrow shoulder of rocky land between the bulk of Mount Mycale (*below right*) and cliffs that dropped steeply to the plain.

With the citizens' comfort in mind, the town was oriented to the south. In the winter, the sun's low-angled rays warmed the meeting places and sitting rooms, but in the summer high-angled rays hit only the roofs. Although the terrain was sloping and asymmetrical, the planners adopted the grid system, popularized in the previous century by Hippodamus, an architect from neighboring Miletus. Seven main roads running east-west intersect at right angles with 15 side streets running north-south. In many places, the slope is so steep that the side streets rise in steps.

The highest spot in the city was reserved for a temple dedicated to the goddess Athena, doubtless because Priene's orig-

126

inal settlers came from Athens. The temple was laid out by the Carian architect Pytheos, who earlier had designed the Mausoleum at Halicarnassus, another of the Seven Wonders of the World. Recognized for its fine scale and beauty, Priene's temple became even more famous after Pytheos published a book on architectural design and used the temple as the model of Ionic construction. Of the building's original 38 columns, five stand today *(below)*.

While many of the Ionic cities prospered into Roman times, Priene went into decline, probably in part because of competition from its powerful neighbor Miletus. As a result, the city was never Romanized architecturally. The Priene of

350 BC lingers to this day, much of its original Hellenistic form intact. Thanks to the relative completeness of the ruins, a German architect working from the reports of the German excavators could create the model above encompassing 30 percent of Priene in its heyday. The

gymnasium and stadium can be seen in the foreground. Behind them are blocks of houses, backed by the marketplace and Sacred Stoa, a wide colonnade for promenading. To the left rear is the temple of Athena, and in the center background, the theater.

Bigger than life, this lion was "carved most realistically from the best-quality marble," as one of the ancient sources put it, and once stood on the roof of the Mausoleum at Halicarnassus. The monumental proportions of the tomb and the quality of its sculpted decoration helped establish its reputation as one of the Seven Wonders.

the third wave of immigrants, the Dorians. They claimed descent from the invading Greek peoples who ancient writers reported were responsible for the fall of Mycenae. The Dorians erected bases on the islands of Rhodes and Cos but also built two important colonies on peninsulas extending from the mainland coast, at Cnidos and Halicarnassus. Neither—to judge from excavations—had previously been a regular settlement. Evidence from inscriptions found in the two cities suggests that, in later years at least, the inhabitants maintained very different relations with the local people. While half the proper names listed in Halicarnassian inscriptions are Carian, indicating an ethnically mixed population, almost none of those from Cnidos are; it remained almost exclusively Greek.

Like the Ionians, who founded the Panionian League between the late ninth and early eighth centuries BC, the Dorians established a league called the Hexapolis, in which Cnidos and Halicarnassus joined four centers on the islands to celebrate an annual festival in honor of the god Apollo. The number was reduced to five when Halicarnassus was expelled. According to Herodotus, who was born there in 484 BC, the city's disgrace stemmed from one of its athletes taking home a prize he won at the festival games, instead of dedicating it to the deity in the local temple as custom demanded.

The anecdote demonstrates that the Greek cities, though scattered along the coast, shared a common culture and lifestyle. Typically, each community had a citadel, or acropolis, sited for protection on a prominent hill; a theater and a stadium; a gymnasium containing space for indoor exercise and lecture rooms for educating children; a council chamber; several temples; and an agora, a marketplace where people could both haggle and trade and air opinions on matters of common concern.

The first settlers lived mainly by farming, fishing, herding an-

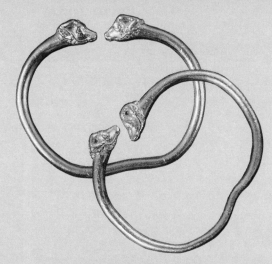

Antelope heads grace the ends of these gold bracelets found on the wrists of the skeleton—which was sprinkled with hundreds of bits of gold appliqué that had adorned the burial gown.

The floral motif of the crown is repeated by the bud-shaped beads of the gold necklace above. A portrait of the god Apollo decorates the gold and agate ring at right.

Found between the burial chamber's stone wall and the foot of the sarcophagus, this black-glazed oinochoe, or wine decanter, is about 6½ inches tall, and may have been the queen's favorite. Similar vessels found elsewhere have been conclusively dated to the time of the Carian queen Ada.

lennium BC, and that a people lived there later who traded with the Trojans to the north as well as with the Hittites to the east.

As revealed by the great quantity of protogeometric pottery the archaeologists unearthed, the first Greek colonists, the Aeolians, arrived in the 10th century BC. They established themselves on a small promontory linked by a causeway to the mainland, and they equipped their single-room mud-brick cottages with vents to allow smoke to escape through their thatched roofs. Conditions improved in the following century, when the island site was flattened and the settlement was extended to house as many as 500 families behind a substantial wall. Herodotus wrote that refugees from the Ionian colony of Colophon sought asylum in the enlarged city 100 years later, only to seize it when its Aeolian inhabitants were celebrating a religious festival beyond its walls.

Ionian Smyrna flourished, sharing in the general prosperity of the eighth century BC. Most of the ancient Greeks believed that Homer himself was born there. To judge from signs of fire damage found by the excavators, much of the existing port was burned down around the year 700 BC, but old Smyrna was quickly rebuilt to a more systematic plan and given a splendid new temple dedicated to the goddess Athena that Akurgal has described as "the earliest and finest religious building of the eastern Greek world in Asia Minor."

Though ancient Smyrna's history might seem eventful enough, it took another dramatic turn soon after 600 BC, when the city became the principal casualty of a Lydian assault on the coast. The effects of the raid were so devastating that Smyrna did not regain its former importance until the city was moved to another site three centuries later. In the meantime, according to Strabo, it "was inhabited village-fashion." The diggers have found evidence of continued occupation, but the town regained municipal status only in 334 BC, when it was refounded by Alexander the Great to the south of Bayrakli, on the slopes of Mount Pagos, where the city of Smyrna, or present-day Izmir, now stands. At this location grew up what Strabo, writing around the end of the first century BC, would call the finest Ionian city of his day.

Miletus, which had been under attack from the time of the first Lydian king, was said to have endured 11 years of annual hostile raids before the Lydians, acting on the words of the oracle at Delphi,

A color-coded satellite image of the Xan-thus River, seen as a blue line snaking from the upper left to center, illustrates the extent of silting in coastal Lycia. In about 500 BC the continental shelf sank, creating a depression marked by the red triangle. Silt washed down by rain from the highlands—where trees had been clear-cut—and borne to the sea by the riv-er gradually filled up the lowlands, bury-ing most signs of human habitation un-der 10 feet of mud. The silting process con-tinues today: The dark blue triangle identifies new deposits carried into the black-tinted Mediterranean.

made peace. By then the city, located on a headland at the mouth of a gulf, was outgrowing its resources and had spearheaded a move-ment to send colonists to the Sea of Marmara, between the Dar-danelles and the Bosporus, and eventually to the Black Sea coast. The first such settlement was established—with the permission of the Lydian king—at Abydus, less than 20 miles northeast of Troy. Fur-ther foundations were soon set up on the coast of the Sea of Mar-mara before the Bosporus was breached and large-scale colonization of the Black Sea coast began. Ultimately Miletus was said, perhaps with some exaggeration, to have been the mother of 90 colonies.

At home, Milesians pioneered exploration of a different sort. The city was the cradle of Greek physical science. Perhaps its most in-fluential thinker was Thales, whose speculations on the nature of matter led him to the conclusion that water was the basic element of existence. He also won fame for more practical intellectual feats, in-cluding calculating the height of the Egyptian pyramids from the length of the shadows they cast and predicting an eclipse of the sun.

Tired of answering critics who complained that he was overly concerned with abstract matters, he once demonstrated the practical uses of his scholarship by renting all the city's olive presses ahead of the harvest. His knowledge of astronomy had led him to foresee a good olive crop that year, and when it came in as he had predicted he was able to advance the cause of philosophy by making a killing.

Alone among the Greek cities on Anatolia's mainland, Miletus held out against the Persians for a generation. And when it came under imperial sway, its people proved unwilling subjects. In 499 BC they spearheaded the ill-fated Ionian revolt against Achaemenid rule. Other cities rallied to the cause, and Athens sent a small fleet.

At first the rebels were successful, sacking Sardis and burning all of the town but the acropolis, where the Persian garrison held out, but it was to prove an expensive victory for Miletus. When the revolt was crushed five years later, most of Miletus's men were killed, and the women and children were enslaved. The few males who survived were taken as prisoners to Susa and later resettled at Ampe, almost 2,000 miles away at the head of the Persian Gulf, where Darius I reckoned to put their maritime skills at the service of his navy. The disaster caused such anguish in Greece that when a tragedy called *The Capture of Miletus* was staged in Athens, the audience burst into tears and the playwright was fined for upsetting public order. A law was soon passed forbidding anyone to perform the work again.

But Miletus survived and even regained much of its importance, despite silting, which has since stranded it nearly five miles inland. Yet in the fourth century BC, it was overshadowed by Halicarnassus, 40 miles south, which had fallen

High above a coastal plain in what was eastern Lycia, Austrian excavators restore the heroön, or shrine, of King Pericles (below). Ruling from the city of Limyra at the foot of the hill, this energetic Anatolian, seen on the coin above, successfully balanced the opposing powers of his day: Though bearing the name of the Greek leader and hero who resisted the Persians, he served as the dynast of the Persian overlords. The 34-by-22-foot shrine was built after his death, around 325 BC.

A Turkish military helicopter—employed in 1994 by Austrian excavators to transport statues and friezes from Limyra's acropolis to the Lower City—lifts off with a crated treasure. The figures had been damaged by earthquake and fire. After restoration they will be permanently displayed in the museum at Antalya.

into the hands of a Carian dynasty that was to show how much could be achieved by cooperation, not conflict, with the Persian empire.

In the Halicarnassian dynasty kingship descended through the female line, so the only way a king's son could become eligible for the throne was by marrying his sister. This the city's best-known ruler, Mausolus, duly did in 377 BC. Mausolus, like his predecessors, was content to hold his realm in the name of the Achaemenids, ruling nominally as a Persian satrap, or provincial governor. In practice he was allowed almost total autonomy, which he used to embark on an ambitious program of Hellenization.

Mausolus decided to make Halicarnassus his capital and the showpiece of his modernization program. All the inhabitants of several smaller towns were compelled to relocate to it, increasing its population four- or fivefold. He also had other Greek-type cities built on the Bodrum peninsula for inland Carians, many of them herdsmen, and to ensure that no residents returned to their former homes, set up police posts or watchtowers in the old settlements.

When Mausolus died in 353 BC, his sister-queen Artemisia remained so devoted to her cremated brother's memory that she is said to have added a pinch of his ashes to her daily glass of wine. She also decided to build the great funerary complex and wonder that became known as the Mausoleum *(pages 128-129)* in his honor. The building rose in statue-lined tiers to a roof topped by a team of four drawing a chariot that may have stood 140 feet above ground—about the height of an 11-story building.

The monument later fell victim to an earthquake and was finally demolished by the crusader Knights of Saint John in the 15th century, who used the stone to build the castle of Bodrum. Charles Newton, an assistant curator of the British Museum, found much of the little that remained— 66 statues or fragments of statuary—and transferred the pieces to London in the 1850s.

The west coast's other wonder, the Temple of Artemis, or the Artemision, at Ephesus, suffered an equally inglorious fate. It disappeared entirely, its stone used partly in the construction of the Church of Saint John on the slope above the site, and its paltry remains were overwhelmed by silting. Yet, in its day—which lasted up to the triumph of Christianity in the fourth century AD—the Artemision reigned supreme among the sacred sites of Anatolia.

This finely executed head comes from a Lycian tomb and is probably a portrait of the occupant, whose name has been lost. He was interred around 475 BC in a rectangular, stone-lined chamber cut into a mountainside above the plain of Elmali.

The veneration of Artemis had roots reaching far back in time, well before the age of Greek colonization. According to both Strabo and Pausanias, the city's first Ionian settlers took over the mother-goddess cult of the local Anatolians. Recent discoveries of Mycenaean pottery in the area suggest that there might even have been Greek contact with a cult center there in the Bronze Age.

The earliest temple of Artemis may have already existed in the eighth century BC but was destroyed by the Cimmerians, nomadic raiders from the Caucasus region. The great building that replaced it—the first temple to be built entirely of marble and one of the two biggest edifices ever erected in the Greek world, the second being an even larger version of the same—was still under construction at the time of the Lydian conquest in the sixth century BC. So fervent was the Ephesians' belief in the powers of the goddess that they tried to put their city under her protection by running a rope from the unfinished temple to the town, about three-quarters of a mile away. But their efforts yielded mixed results: Croesus, the Lydian king, destroyed the city and transplanted its residents, but he spared the sanctuary, which he generously endowed; 19th-century excavators uncovered fragments of columns with his name inscribed upon them. The building was ravaged two centuries later by a fire set by a madman named Herostratus who hoped in so doing—with some success, as it turned out—to make his name live in history.

The disaster had an unexpected sequel, for it turned out that Alexander the Great had been born in 356 BC on the day of the fire. The conqueror was sufficiently impressed by the coincidence to vow to rebuild the temple on an even more magnificent scale when he came to the city 22 years later, decreeing that the annual taxes that Ephesus had previously paid to the Persians be devoted to that purpose. The structure that rose from the ashes was modeled closely on the design of its predecessor.

The city flourished along with its temple, particularly after Lysimachus, one of Alexander's generals and successors, determined to overcome the perennial problem of silting by rebuilding Ephesus on a new site more than a mile seaward of the sanctuary. To persuade unwilling citizens to leave their old homes, he reportedly blocked the drains, flooding them out in a tide of sewage.

The fine new metropolis he created was eventually to become the capital of the Roman province of Asia, with a population of perhaps 250,000. Saint Paul preached there, starting a riot among the city's silversmiths, who feared that the new faith he brought would threaten the lucrative trade in images associated with Artemis that formed the major part of their livelihood. Ac-

The Nereid Monument is considered the most Greek of the Lycian tombs. With the permission of the Turkish sultan, Charles Fellows took it to the British Museum in 1842, where it stands today. The billowy female figures between the columns are thought to be Nereids—amiable nymphs, kindly to sailors, and daughters of Nereus, the wise old man of the sea.

cording to an ancient tradition, it was to Ephesus too that Saint John brought the Virgin Mary after the Crucifixion.

The other great eastern Greek center of the period after Alexander was Pergamon. It too owed much of its rise to Lysimachus, who made it the depository of his treasury. When the general died in battle in 281 BC, the man charged with guarding the money used it to embellish the city and passed it on to his adopted son Eumenes, who is considered to be the first king of Pergamon. Its greatest ruler, Attalus I, won a great victory over the Galatians—Celtic mercenaries who had established themselves in Asia Minor—in 230 BC. Thereafter his Attalid successors allied themselves with the rising power of Rome, receiving in return control over much of western Asia Minor.

Claiming to be the spiritual heirs of classical Greek culture, the Attalids won a reputation as patrons of the arts. They decorated their capital with magnificent new buildings, and under their patronage Pergamon became one of the greatest trading centers of Asia Minor. A fine example of Hellenistic city planning, it occupied a site that has been called the most impressive of any of the cities in the region, rising in semicircular terraces up a slope between two tributaries of the Caicus River. The plan offered spectacular vistas both to view-

More than 2,000 years ago tombs like these—with facades in the style of Ionic temples—were carved directly into the living rock above the Carian city of Caunus. They exhibit the Greek influence of the fourth century BC. Although they originally overlooked the Mediterranean, as the result of silting they now lie 2½ miles from the shore. The Carians were one of the native Anatolian peoples who for thousands of years built architecturally distinctive tombs for themselves.

This limestone sarcophagus, constructed in Xanthus in about 375 BC for a man named Payava, stands 20 feet tall. It is richly decorated: Projecting beams imitate wooden construction; lions' heads jut from the roof; and friezes illustrate both Greek and Persian themes.

138

ers looking down from on high and to those gazing up from below.

The city's pride was its library. Lacking the papyrus reeds used to make the scrolls familiar in Egypt, its scribes used untanned animal hides that were treated with lime to loosen the hairs, then scraped, stretched, and finally rubbed with chalk and pumice. The resulting leaves—called parchment from the name of the city—could be stitched together to form paged books. The collection assembled by the kings rivaled that of Alexandria in Egypt, and by a twist of fate Alexandria was where it was to end up, offered as a gift to the Egyptian queen Cleopatra by her Roman lover, Mark Antony, when he found himself in control of Asia during the second Triumvirate.

The city's other famous monuments were the spectacular theater, which rises 78 rows high and has 10,000 seats, and the celebrated Great Altar of Zeus, set in a colonnaded court laid out on a podium that was approached by a ceremonial staircase 66 feet broad. The altar site was excavated by a young German engineer, Carl Humann, in the late 19th century. He recovered most of a great frieze depicting a battle between the gods and the giants, and sent it back to Berlin, where it became the centerpiece of the German capital's Pergamon Museum.

The later discovery of a remarkable stone inscription detailing some of the city's bylaws offers a vivid glimpse of daily life on the Anatolian coast more than two millennia ago. Fines were levied for householders who threw refuse out of doors, dug up roads in search of gravel or stones, or let wastepipes discharge above ground rather than underground into the public drains. People who left obstructions in the roadway were typically charged the costs of removal plus 50 percent.

Pergamon's last independent ruler, Attalus III, maintained the city's intellectual tradition in a markedly eccentric way. A reclusive scholar, he devoted much of his energy to science, and in particular the study of poisonous plants, whose effects he used to test on condemned criminals. He died heirless in 133 BC and to the astonishment of his subjects bequeathed the state in his will to the Romans. Three years later, after putting down a rebellion led by an illegitimate son of a former king, the Romans duly incorporated the kingdom, which by then included much of the west coast, into their empire as the newly created province of Asia. In the centuries of imperial rule that ensued, many of the coastal cities reached new peaks of prosperity and were adorned with fine new buildings, but they never regained the intellectual preeminence that they had attained in earlier days.

As the Roman tide swept down the west coast, only Lycia at its southernmost extremity continued to hold out. The region had always been fiercely independent, protected from incursions both by its geography and by the spirit of its people. It was a country of large forests and snowy peaks, some rising to 10,000 feet. In many areas the mountains extended to the coast, falling away to the sea in precipitous cliffs. Its main cities were along the shore or in the fertile valley of the Xanthus River, which ran through the Lycian heartland and was the site of the region's largest city, also called Xanthus. The country's population is thought not to have exceeded 200,000 people.

The inhabitants of this rugged land seem to have descended from west Anatolians of the Bronze Age. They can probably be identified with the Lukka, a people who were conquered by the Hittite kings in the mid-14th century BC but who proved unwilling subjects, often rising in revolt. The Lukka were mariners who raided Cyprus and are said to have conspired with the Libyans and the Sea Peoples as they made the first of their two attempts to invade Egypt in 1220 BC, only to be repulsed by the pharaoh Merenptah. (The second assault, around 1200 BC, would be stopped by Ramses III.)

Homer knew the Lukka by their more modern name of Lycians, and they play a significant part in the *Iliad,* fighting courageously with the Trojans against the Mycenaean Greeks. To judge from the archaeological evidence, the first Greek colonists in the Lycians' area, the Dorians from Rhodes, seem to have penetrated Lycian lands from about 700 BC on, controlling an island off the main coast but managing to set up only a single, isolated colony at Phaselis on their eastern borders. Elsewhere, however, the native population preserved the country's territorial integrity.

Lycia was the only region of western Anatolia to hold out against the Lydians under King Croesus. It did succumb to the Persians, but only after a ferocious battle at Xanthus, whose defenders chose to burn down their citadel with their own wives and children

HELLENISM ON A GRAND SCALE

Were it not for the extraordinary hubris of one ordinary ruler, the Anatolian area once known as Commagene would probably be one of history's forgotten kingdoms. As it is, the colossal limestone statues atop Nemrud Dagh in southeast Turkey that Antiochus I built to honor himself and his ancestors stand as a monument not just to supreme ego but to the grand influence of Hellenism.

Persian by birth and the son of a king, Antiochus nevertheless felt compelled to incorporate Greek culture into his grandiose work. Greek inscriptions adorn the statues and describe hybrid Greek-Persian gods who populate the east and west terraces of the mountaintop: Zeus-Ahura Mazda, Apollo-Mithra, Heracles-Verethragna. Antiochus even claimed joint ancestry with the Greeks, through Alexander the Great on his mother's side.

About all that remains intact of Antiochus's monument is the guardian eagle shown at left, which sits alone on the north terrace, peering out over the now-arid landscape. The eagle, a persistent symbol throughout Anatolia and ancient Mesopotamia, is a fitting ornament for this abandoned sanctuary, where one finds the religion, art, and politics of West and East as jumbled as the earthquake-wrecked stones themselves.

The toppled head of Apollo, almost 10 feet tall, and the head of a guardian eagle stare out from the west terrace of Nemrud Dagh. Apollo is outfitted with a Persian-style miter, or turban. The row of now-headless gods enthroned on the platform of the east terrace (inset) once rose five stories high.

At far right, Zeus, the inspiration for the monument, looms in front of Antiochus I, the builder. Antiochus wrote on the base of one of the statues that his altar was at the "topmost ridge" of his kingdom, "in closest proximity to the heavenly throne of Zeus." In the inset, Antiochus's father, on the left, greets Heracles. The style of the relief and the poses of the subjects show still another cultural influence—Hittite.

in it rather than see the city—and their loved ones—fall into the hands of the invaders. They then went down fighting to the last man. Their successors put up similarly uncompromising resistance to the Roman general Brutus 500 years later, when barely 150 people survived a siege of the city, many of the others dying by their own hands.

The Lycian language is known through a relatively large corpus of inscriptions, most of them funerary texts from tombs that members of the upper class built for themselves and their families. Related to Luwian, a second-millennium Anatolian tongue of Indo-European stock, it was set down in an alphabet that borrowed most of its characters from Dorian Greek. Never a popular form of writing, and usually accompanied in inscriptions by Greek or Aramaic, the tongue seems to have died out in the third century BC, when Greek became the lingua franca of the ancient world.

The tombs *(pages 138-139)* themselves are the Lycians' best-known monuments. Some, reckoned the earliest, have a form that is peculiar to the region, consisting of a rectangular pillar surmounted by a grave chamber. Others—carved into cliff faces—take the form of houses and preserve for scholars a clear image of native building styles, the residences themselves having been built of perishable wood, plentifully available from the region's extensive forests.

Xanthus proved a rich source of antiquities when it was visited in 1838 by the English scholar Sir Charles Fellows. His journals attracted so much interest that a British naval vessel was dispatched to the site and returned with more than 70 huge crates of carvings. In London the sculptures caused almost as much of a stir as the Elgin Marbles had 40 years earlier, and the Xanthian Room in which they are exhibited remains a popular attraction of the British Museum.

Since 1950, French teams have excavated Xanthus and sites nearby, while Turkish investigators have been digging at the harbor town of Patara. The use of timber as the principal building material has restricted the extent of the findings, but the archaeologists have nonetheless been able to trace the growth of the city, which expanded tremendously in Hellenistic times, and to uncover evidence of damage to the citadel dating back to the time of the Persian siege. Two and a half miles to the southwest, archaeologists have also explored the remains of a sanctuary that included a celebrated temple dedicated to the goddess Leto, the mother of Apollo and Artemis. There they found large numbers of terra-cotta figurines that had apparently been thrown into a sacred spring as an offering to the deity.

This sensuous terra-cotta statue of Aphrodite, the goddess of love, was made in the Aeolian city of Myrina about 150 BC. She is looking to the right, perhaps at Eros; in her missing left hand she may have held a mirror. This representation of the erotic side of woman complements Anatolia's better-known tradition of depicting her as a child-bearing or reverential figure.

The end of Lycia as an independent entity came in AD 43, when the emperor Claudius took direct control of its cities. Yet the region continued to play an important role in Roman times. Myra and its port of Andriace, for example, rose to prominence as one of the main points where Egyptian grain was transshipped on its way to Rome, and it was at the harbor that Saint Paul changed ships when he was sent under arrest from Jerusalem to Rome. Later still it was to be the seat of Saint Nicholas, a fourth-century-AD bishop of the city who found posthumous fame as Santa Claus.

In the long peace of Roman times, the independent spirit of the western Anatolian peoples gradually waned. Yet Hellenism, the imaginative spark that inspired the Anatolian Greeks' notions of art, religion, architecture, and politics, had already made itself felt over a wide area. Spread to neighboring countries and beyond by traders and sailors, observed and imitated by indigenous peoples and wayfarers, and then borne in the wake of Alexander's armies, Hellenistic culture had taken root in distant lands less through force of arms than for the evident advantages it brought with it. Quite simply, it provided a model for civilized urban living that, within the limitations of a pretechnological age, could hardly be bettered.

As it traveled eastward, however, Hellenism underwent a subtle process of change. Fulfilling its historic destiny, Anatolia served as a meeting place of East and West. Of all the odd marriages between European and Asian ways that were forged over the succeeding centuries, few can have been more extravagant than one whose surviving monuments can be seen today on a mountaintop in the Anti-Taurus range, 34 miles northeast of Samosata, the ancient capital of the almost-forgotten kingdom of Commagene in eastern Turkey. Here, on the summit of Nemrud Dagh—literally, Mount Nimrod—colossal heads of a king and Persian and Greek gods and heroes lie toppled side by side, the shattered remains of a sculpted pantheon in which Zeus was identified with the Persian deity Ahura Mazda and Apollo with Mithra *(pages 141-145)*.

First excavated by German and Turkish archaeologists in the 1880s, the monuments of Nemrud Dagh were reexamined in 1953 by a team sponsored by the American Schools of Oriental Research and led by American scholar Theresa Goell. The site proved a difficult one. Fetching water involved a three-hour round trip, and the nearest substantial village at that time was two days' journey away. In the midday sun the temperature rose to 130°F.; at night it sank to freezing. Driving rain, thunderstorms, and billowing dust provided additional hazards, as did roving bears.

Working under these conditions, Goell and her assistants recorded and investigated the site and confirmed that it had been built as the intended burial place of Antiochus I, the ruler of Commagene. This small but wealthy state, commanding an important trade route across the Euphrates River, broke away from the Seleucid empire of Alexander's Asian heirs sometime in the second century BC. It survived to become a buffer state between Rome and Parthia before finally being incorporated into the Roman Empire in AD 72. Antiochus, who is said to have died in either AD 32 or 34, had declared himself to be a god sometime before his demise. The mountaintop tomb he prepared for himself was intended to be worthy of his immortal peers.

His workers cut three platforms on the peak's summit, the "topmost ridge" in the kingdom, as an inscription reads. From the debris they made a funeral cairn 150 feet high, beneath which, it is assumed, the king's body was laid to rest in a yet-undiscovered chamber. One of the terraces served as a gateway to the sanctuary. It was left unadorned, save for a sculpted eagle and a wall of standing slabs. The other two held arrays of sculptures, each as tall as a two-story house, representing the monarch and his gods and rows of reliefs of his forebears. Antiochus traced his descent on the male side from the Achaemenid rulers of Persia and on the female from Alexander the Great, a doubly imperial inheritance that explains the strange mixture of divinities in whose company he chose to take his rest.

Earthquakes and erosion have long since toppled most of the statues, leaving a surrealistic jumble of headless torsos and colossal visages to share the king's final resting place. Yet in their oddity and grandeur, they provide a fitting monument not just to the overweening ambition of one petty ruler but to ancient Anatolia itself. Anatolia was long known only through the eyes of the classical historians as a land of half-legendary rulers and fabulous treasures. Now it stands revealed by archaeologists and scholars as an extraordinary cultural melting pot, where European, Asian, and Anatolian civilizations came together to produce much that was rich and wondrous.

TEMPLES OF VANISHED DREAMS

Two columns of the Temple of Apollo at Didyma soar toward the heavens as they did 2,000 years ago. Even in its ruined state, this great building speaks eloquently of the past, and its inner court seems still to echo with the pronouncements of the oracles who presided there. Throughout Anatolia there are other, similar Greek and Roman holy sites to which visitors from all over the Mediterranean world flocked by the thousand in an effort to gain some control over their lives. Often, these places were associated with water—sacred springs bubbling up from deep within the earth that were thought to bear the messages of subterranean powers.

Some holy sites date back thousands of years, when shrines and temples grew up around the springs, and men and women with the gift of prophecy began interpreting the messages for the edification of the needy.

The fame of these places and their oracles soon spread, and the temples grew ever bigger on the fees charged the so-called consultants—questers after certitude, good health, and well-being.

Chief among the deities celebrated at such centers of religion and magic was the Greek god Apollo. He was venerated, among other things, as the god of prophecy and healing and as the father of Asklepios, the god of medicine. The cult of Apollo may have arisen in Anatolia, but his most famous oracular shrine was at Delphi in Greece. There, a middle-aged prophetess dressed as a young virgin sat on a tripod and breathed in the fumes of chopped bay leaves, hemp, and barley burning over an oil fire. The resulting high, it was believed, put her in touch with Apollo—something the travelers to the Anatolian sites covered in this essay hoped to achieve for themselves.

A CENTER OF HEALING

The base of an altar at the Asklepion is decorated with olive garlands, rosettes, and snakes. Seeming to renew themselves annually by shedding their skin, snakes became associated with both Apollo and Asklepios, who were noted for their powers of rejuvenation.

A famed place of healing, the Asklepion lay at the foot of the acropolis on which the proud city of Pergamon stood. Here people came to have their ailments cured. As the aerial photograph below shows, facilities were elaborate. They included temples dedicated to Asklepios, a library, a colonnaded walkway, and a 3,500-seat theater.

Among the treatments were mud baths, colonics, herbal remedies, exercise, special diets, therapeutic drama, and dream analysis. God-inspired dreams were considered essential to cures. Incubants, as the patients were called, would be ushered into the temple at night, allotted pallets on which to sleep, and invited to dream. For some, there were miraculous cures. But for others less lucky, the night visions required interpretation; to this end the incubants discussed the dreams among themselves and with the priests, coming up with prescriptions to follow.

A second-century-AD visitor, Aelius Aristedes, wrote a book about his dreams. Whenever the god intervened directly upon his behalf, Aristedes found "salvation, strength, comfort, ease, high spirits, and every good thing." But he kept coming back over a 13-year period, suggesting that like his dreams, the cures were short-lived.

This circular subterranean chamber in the so-called Therapy Building connected to an underground passage that led to the sacred spring at the center of the complex. People drank the mildly radioactive water and bathed in it, seeking relief from a variety of ailments.

Evidence of cures, the eyes and ear below, which are made of bronze, were left to express the gratitude of two patients. The bronze serpent above is a reminder that the snake was a sacred animal of both Apollo and Asklepios. Live snakes were kept at the Asklepion; it was said that a blind person who was licked on the eye by a snake would have his sight restored.

THE SEAT OF PROPHECY

Thanks to a succession of oracles, the Temple of Apollo at Didyma enjoyed a long reputation that rivaled that of the shrine at Delphi. From ancient times to 494 BC, all of the oracles had been men, members of the Branchidae family, descended from a handsome shepherd with whom Apollo had fallen in love and on whom the god bestowed the gift of prophecy. Then, in 494 BC, after the defeat by the Persians of the temple's protectors, the Milesians, the Branchidae were exiled to Central Asia, and the temple was looted and burned. Some 150 years later the local inhabitants began rebuilding it and installed a female line of seers.

Just how the oracles operated, no one knows. Doubtless, they used in their ritual the spring that rose in the courtyard of the inner sanctum. And it is likely that they fell into a trance or became possessed, thus able to receive divine messages. But the discovery in 1901 of a bronze knucklebone *(far right)* suggests that they may also have resorted to casting lots. This object, one of a pair from a satisfied consultant, as visitors were known then, may well represent the knucklebones—forerunners of dice—employed by Greeks and Romans in games of chance. At Didyma, the bones were probably marked Yes or No. The consultant posed a direct question, the oracle tossed them, and the answer appeared.

Once positioned high on the temple's facade, this Medusa head is now at ground level. The wall around the inner sanctum (below), *seen here restored to one-third its original height, rose 80 feet. The enormous temple, with columns 60 feet high, measured 384 feet in length and 195 in width.*

Columns rise from an elevated marble platform at the front of the temple. The door to the rear is one of two giving access to passages leading to the sunken courtyard and sacred spring.

More than 12 inches wide, 8 inches high, and weighing slightly less than 200 pounds, this bronze replica of a knucklebone—a thank offering—was taken to Persia in 494 BC by soldiers as war booty. The inscription supplies the donor's and caster's names.

The two sloping passages leading, like this one, from the outside of the temple to the courtyard, were deliberately made narrow. Not wide enough for two individuals to walk abreast, the pathways forced select visitors to enter the high-walled, roofless inner sanctum single file, adding to the awe that coming into the presence of the oracle must have inspired.

TEMPLE OF MYSTERIES

Smaller by far than the temple at Didyma, the Temple of Apollo at Claros nevertheless developed a strong reputation during Anatolia's Roman period. Indeed, it became such an attraction that no less a figure than Germanicus Caesar, the adoptive son of the emperor Tiberius, paid it a visit. The process of divination is described by the historian Tacitus, who relates how the oracle, "after departing into a grotto and taking a draught of water from a hidden spring, produces replies in set forms of verses on the subject which each enquirer has conceived in his mind."

Some years later the historian Pliny the Elder noted that, although consuming the water enabled the oracle to produce "marvelous prophecies," it was an act not without risk, since the water was certain to shorten "the life of the drinker."

Externally, the temple resembled other such classical structures, but unlike them it had an unusual basement, in which the sacred spring was located. Two stairways of four steps each descended into this low-ceilinged netherworld. A passage, so narrow it forced the consultants to proceed single file, led directly under the middle of the temple to a kind of waiting room that contained a marble bench. Beyond lay another passage, to be used only by the oracle, who followed it to reach a chamber where a well contained the miracle-working water.

Found under the oldest altar of Apollo at Claros in 1992, this bronze pendant represents the Egyptian crocodile god Sobek. It may have been brought back from Egypt by an Anatolian mercenary as an offering. Below, part of a cult statue of Artemis, Apollo's twin sister, lies on the temple floor.

A rising water table has left the basement of the temple partially submerged. Although an earthquake during the Middle Ages is supposed to have laid flat the part of the building above ground, the basement survived undamaged, gradually filling with flood-borne silt. The vaults helped support the weight of large cult statues in the temple proper.

Though no oracular messages survive at Claros, the names of visitors do, as on the column at right. Such inscriptions appear on steps and elsewhere around the temple grounds, a unique feature. Some are lists of choristers who came here to celebrate rites associated with Apollo. This temple, and the one at Didyma, closed in the third century BC as Christianity triumphed over paganism.

HOME TO THE GODDESS

Once one of the Seven Wonders of the World, the Artemision *(below)* presents a sorry sight at the close of the 20th century, with only a lone column and some masonry to hint at its former grandeur. Here also rose a sacred spring, but the greater attraction was a statue of Artemis, the mother goddess, that stood imposingly within the main chamber. Although the original was destroyed long ago, life-size Roman adaptations, like the one shown on the opposite page, give an impression of what the work must have looked like.

Artemis had a long evolution, from the plump Anatolian mother goddess of the Neolithic period, through her local transformation into Kybele, to her eventual Roman incarnation as Diana. The temple site lies close to Ephesus, the city where Saint Paul preached and, local belief holds, Saint John the Apostle accompanied the Virgin Mary after the Ascension of Jesus. In addition, legend has it that Mary died in the vicinity.

Once Chrisianity gained the upper hand in the region, the temple was stripped of many of its stones so that the Church of Saint John, seen crowning the hill below, on the left, could be built in the sixth century AD. Some years earlier, a gathering of early church fathers convening at Ephesus officially sanctioned the Cult of the Virgin, whose members were already worshiping Mary as the Mother of God.

The four-inch-tall gold priestess shown below was left at the temple as a votive offering. The priestess wears a beatific smile as an idolator of Artemis, who was not only the mother goddess but the queen of all the animals.

Flanked by deer and beehives, Artemis stretches out her arms in this second-century-AD Roman sculpture. In addition to an animal-ornamented headdress and skirt, her attire includes a necklace beneath which can be seen the signs of the zodiac, and a vest from which protrude symbols of fertility—perhaps breasts, fruit, eggs, or even bull's testes.

LAYERS OF HISTORY WHERE EAST MEETS WEST

Jutting out of Asia and straining toward Europe, the Anatolian landmass has long served as a bridge between the two continents, absorbing the influences of both—and producing distinct cultures of its own. And while today the majority of its people are Sunni Muslim and speak Turkish, Anatolia is a region with a great multilayered, multicultural past.

This "land of dreams," as Homer called it, has a history that often blends fact with myth. In the far east, amid the mountain ranges of Armenia, towers Mount Ararat, reputed resting place of Noah's Ark after the Flood. On Anatolia's western shores, just miles from Europe, stood Troy, site of the legendary Trojan War. And to the north, along the coast of the Black Sea, lay the fabled land of the Amazons, the mythical tribe of female warriors.

Perched at a historic crossroads between East and West, Anatolia has always drawn successive waves of newcomers. Threading through the mountains to reach its sheltered valleys, or sailing the Mediterranean, Aegean, and Black Seas to its fertile coastal regions, outsiders have founded new civilizations here or made the land part of larger empires.

But before this, reaching back to the Paleolithic, or Old Stone Age, Anatolia's peoples began to leave evidence of their presence, in the form of flint hand axes, scrapers, and other tools. And at a time when most Europeans were still food-gathering cave dwellers, Anatolians began to develop settled and partially agricultural communities, using techniques that would eventually take root in Europe itself.

NEOLITHIC AND CHALCOLITHIC AGES 8000–3000 BC

FERTILITY FIGURE FROM CHATAL HÖYÜK

During the Neolithic era, or New Stone Age, humans first began to change from a seminomadic life of hunting and gathering to a more settled lifestyle based on the rearing of animals and the harvesting of crops. Among the first places to make this transition was southern Anatolia, where settlements like Chayönü near the foothills of the Taurus Mountains thrived on the cultivation of wheat, peas, and lentils, and on the domestication of sheep and pigs. But the height of Neolithic culture in Anatolia is found at Chatal Höyük, which was a flourishing township by 6000 BC and developed into one of the world's first cities. Religion seems to have been an important part of life for the 5,000 to 10,000 people of Chatal Höyük. The mother-goddess figure above, found in the city, was the dominant entity in the Neolithic pantheon.

Although Chatal Höyük was abandoned around the middle of the sixth millennium BC, other communities spread across Anatolia, especially when the Neolithic gave way to the Chalcolithic Age (5500-3000 BC) and humans began to use metal in addition to stone. But while contemporary urban areas in Mesopotamia, for example, grew up around a central temple, those in Anatolia were more often connected with a fortress, such as at Hacilar and Mersin, in the south of the country.

BRONZE AGE 3000–1200 BC

HITTITE RHYTON

Early Bronze Age Anatolia experienced a period of great growth, and the land became a patchwork of city-states, the most famous of which was Troy. And around 1950 BC the records of Assyrians trading in Anatolia indicate the increasing importance of a new, Indo-European people. Known as the Hittites, this group would dominate Anatolia for almost 1,000 years.

Humane lawgivers, shrewd diplomats, and gifted metalworkers—as shown by the silver ritual vessel above—the Hittites were most revered as warriors. Landlocked and surrounded by enemies, the Hittites were always at war, battling to hold sway in Anatolia and extend their control south, east, and west through a series of vassal states. By the end of the 14th century BC, they had forged an empire rivaled only by the Egypt of Ramses II. Around 1275 BC the two clashed when the Hittites repulsed an Egyptian advance into northern Syria. Fearful of growing Assyrian strength in the east, however, they eventually concluded a peace treaty with Egypt. But Hittite power was waning. Failing harvests and increasing social instability left the once-great empire unable to resist seafaring invaders from the west who arrived in Anatolia around 1200 BC. These so-called Sea Peoples would sweep all before them until they were halted on the frontiers of Egypt.

IRON AGE
1200–546 BC

PHRYGIAN IVORY STATUETTE

In the wake of the Hittite collapse, new peoples began to enter the land. From the Balkans, the first Phrygian settlers arrived after the 13th century BC, and by about 800 BC the Phrygians had established a unified kingdom in central and western Anatolia. But like the Hittites before them, the Phrygians were boxed in by enemies. After a defeat by Cimmerians sweeping down from the Caucasus around the beginning of the seventh century BC, Phrygian power declined. The kingdom's western possessions came under the hegemony of the Lydian civilization, which made its capital at Sardis.

For more than 100 years, Lydian kings dominated western Anatolia, forming close trading relations with the Greek colonists who had been establishing settlements along the Aegean coast since the 10th century BC. But in the east Lydia was threatened by Medes from Iran, who were pushing through the Armenian mountains, and by the Babylonians, who were moving into the coastal plain south of the Taurus range. After Cyrus I of Persia defeated the Medes in 550 BC, however, Lydia came into conflict with the great rising power in the east. In 546 BC, Cyrus conquered Lydia and incorporated Anatolia into the growing Persian empire.

PERSIAN AND
HELLENISTIC PERIOD
546–30 BC

ALEXANDER THE GREAT

The Persians governed Anatolia from Sardis, which became an important center within their realm. As new masters in the region, they also controlled the Greek cities along the Aegean, whose inhabitants regarded Persian rule as repressive. But Persia had little influence on the local communities, for this period is marked by the advance of Greek civilization. And after the arrival in Asia in 334 BC of Macedonia's Alexander the Great—who is depicted above in a bust from Pergamon—the process of Hellenization was completed.

Although Anatolia fell under Alexander's rule for little more than a decade, his influence on the land was immense. In addition to liberating the population from Persian control, he served as a catalyst in spreading Greek language, literature, and ideas to the neighboring peoples of the interior. After Alexander's death, the history of Anatolia was one of civil war between the kingdoms set up by his successors. In time, these rivalries drew into the region the Romans, who by 146 BC had conquered Greece itself. Although local rulers tried to stem the Roman advance into Anatolia, the country was gradually absorbed over the course of 100 years or so, and the eastern frontier of the Roman Empire was pushed back to the mountains of Armenia and the Euphrates River.

ROMAN PERIOD
30 BC–AD 395

**HADRIAN'S TEMPLE,
EPHESUS**

Under Roman rule, unprecedented security and prosperity were enjoyed by Anatolia, which, as the new imperial province of Asia, became one of the richest parts of the empire. The emperor Hadrian was particularly fond of Ephesus, whose townsfolk dedicated a temple in his honor *(above)*. Hellenism remained strong as well, however, and the Greek language always had more widespread use than Latin. But in the first century AD, a third cultural force began to spread throughout the land.

Born in Roman Palestine, the new religion of Christianity first took hold in Anatolia. Here Paul the Apostle, a native of the southern city of Tarsus, spent most of his early missionary journeys, and here the Gospel writer John lived after the crucifixion of Christ. And from the Aegean island of Patmos another John, author of the apocalyptic Book of Revelation, wrote to the Seven Churches of Asia Minor.

Despite efforts to wipe it out, Christianity spread throughout the empire. In AD 324 the convert Constantine became emperor, established the faith as the state religion, and moved his capital out of pagan Rome. Constantine chose as the site for his new, Christian capital the city of Byzantium, renamed Constantinople, on the Bosporus. For 700 years, Anatolia would be at the heart of the Byzantine empire.

ACKNOWLEDGMENTS

The editors wish to thank the following individuals and institutions for their valuable assistance in the preparation of this volume:

Oğuz Alpözen, Bodrum Museum, Bodrum; Achille Bianchi, Rome; Fritz Blakolmer, Institut für Klassische Archäologie, Universität Vienna; Deanna Cross, The Metropolitan Museum of Art, New York; Kayhan Dörtlük, Antalya Museum, Antalya; Ismet Ediz, Çorum Museum, Çorum; Beatrice Epstein, The Metropolitan Museum of Art, New York; Irmgard Ernstmeier, Munich; Ufuk Esin, University of Istanbul, Istanbul; Brigitte Gaspar, Staatliche Museen zu Berlin, Preussischer Kulturbesitz, Vorderasiatisches Museum, Berlin; Juliette de la Genière, Neuilly, France; Crawford H. Greenewalt Jr., University of California, Berkeley; Lothar Haselberger, University of Pennsylvania, Philadelphia; Harald Hauptmann, Deutsches Archäologisches Institut, Istanbul; Ian Hodder, University of Cambridge, Cambridge, England; Israel Museum, Jerusalem; Jerusalem Bible Lands Museum, Jerusalem; Stefan Karwiese, Osterreichisches Archäologisches Institut, Vienna; Gundela Kaschau, Institut für Ur-und Frühgeschichte, Universität Heidelberg, Heidelberg; Volker Kästner, Staatliche Museen zu Berlin, Preussischer Kulturbesitz, Antikensammlung, Berlin; Hans-Jörg Kellner, Munich; Heidrun Klein, Bildarchiv Preussischer Kulturbesitz, Berlin; Fred S. Kleiner, Archaeological Institute of America, Boston University, Boston; Ellen Kohler, University Museum, University of Pennsylvania, Philadelphia; Emre Kongar, Ministry of Culture, Ankara, Turkey; Christian Le Roy, Université de Paris, I Panthéon-Sorbonne, France; Joachim Marzahn, Deutsche Orient Gesellschaft, Berlin; Machteld J. Mellink, Bryn Mawr College, Bryn Mawr, Pennsylvania; Ahmet Mentes, Istanbul Topkapi Museum, Istanbul; Marie Montembault, Musée du Louvre, Paris; Oscar White Muscarella, The Metropolitan Museum of Art, New York; Mehmet Özdoğan, University of Istanbul, Istanbul; Engin Özgen, Ministry of Culture, Ankara, Turkey; Alpay Pasinli, Istanbul Archaeological Museum, Istanbul; Lino Pellegrini, Milan; John Prag, University of Manchester, Lancashire, England; Jeanne Robert, Paris; Lynn E. Roller, University of California, Davis; Kenneth Sams, University of North Carolina, Chapel Hill; Timurçin Savas, Ministry of Culture, Ankara, Turkey; Wulf Schirmer, Institut für Baugeschichte, Universität Karlsruhe, Karlsruhe, Germany; Geneviève Teissier, Musée du Louvre, Paris; Ilhan Temizsoy, Museum of Anatolian Civilizations, Ankara, Turkey; Klaus Tuchelt, Deutsches Archäologisches Institut, Berlin; Enis Üçboyler, Ephesus Museum, Ephesus; Ahmet Unal, Institut für Assyriologie und Hethitologie, Universität, Munich.

PICTURE CREDITS

The sources for the illustrations that appear in this volume are listed below. Credits from left to right are separated by semicolons; credits from top to bottom are separated by dashes.

Cover: The Metropolitan Museum of Art, gift of Norbert Schimmel Trust, 1989 (1989.281.12)/photograph by Schecter Lee. Background Hirmer Fotoarchiv, Munich. End papers by Paul Breeden. 6: © The British Museum, London. 8: From *Researches in Asia Minor, Pontus, and Admenia, with Some Account of Their Antiquities and Geology*, Vol. 1, by William J. Hamilton, John Murray, Albemarle Street, London, 1842. 9: General Research and Humanities Division, New York Public Library/Astor, Lenox and Tilden Foundations. 13: Gianni Dagli Orti, Paris. 15: British Institute of Archaeology, Ankara (2)—© 1990 Kay Chernush. 16: © The British Museum, London. 17: © The British Museum, London—courtesy the National Portrait Gallery, London. 18, 19: © The British Museum, London, from *Discoveries at Ephesus* by J. T Wood, Longmans, Green and Co., London, 1877. 20, 21: © The British Museum, London. 22: Hirmer Fotoarchiv, Munich. 23: Museum of Anatolian Civilizations, Ankara. 24: Gianni Dagli Orti, Paris. 25, 27: Museum of Anatolian Civilizations, Ankara. 29: Gianni Dagli Orti, Paris. 30, 31: Institut für Ur-und Frühgeschichte, Universität Heidelberg. 32: Ufuk Esin. 33: Ufuk Esin (2)—Aksaray Museum. 34: Mehmet Özdoğan, The University of Istanbul. 35: Hezarfen Foto—Diyarbakir Museum; Mehmet Özdoğan (2)—The University of Chicago. 36: Sonia Halliday Photographs, Weston Turville, Buckinghamshire, England. 37: Museum of Anatolian Civilizations, Ankara (2)—Gianni Dagli Orti, Paris. 38: The Metropolitan Museum of Art, gift of Norbert Schimmel Trust (1989.281.110)/photograph by Schecter Lee. 40: Hirmer Fotoarchiv, Munich. 41: R.M.N., Paris. 43: The Metropolitan Museum of Art, gift of Norbert Schimmel Trust, 1989 (1989.281.10)—National Geographic Image Collection. 45: Peter Neve, Malente. 46: Turtian Birgili. 47: Museum of Anatolian Civilizations, Ankara. 49: Erich Lessing/Art Resource. 50, 51: Eberhard Thiem, Lotus Film, Kaufbeuren/courtesy Archaeological Museum, Ankara (2); Bildarchiv Claus Hansmann, Munich/courtesy Musée du Louvre, Paris. 52: Jürgen Seeher, DAI, Instanbul. 53: Art by John Drummond, Time-Life Books staff/based on a drawing by Boğazköy Archiv, DAI, Berlin. 54: Ashmolean Museum, Oxford. 55: The Walters Art Gallery. 56, 57: Staatliche Museen zu Berlin-Preussischer Kulturbesitz, Vorderasiatisches Museum, photos by Jürgen Liepe. 59: Peter Neve, Malente. 61: Peter Neve, Malente—Deutsches Archäologisches Institut, Bogazköy Archiv, Berlin. 62: Ancient Art and Architecture Collection, London—The Metropolitan Museum of Art, gift of Norbert Schimmel Trust, 1989 (1989.281.12) /photograph by Schecter Lee. 65: Hirmer Fotoarchiv, Munich—reconstruction by R. Naumann from *Der Alte Orient* by W. Orthmann, Propyläen Verlag, Berlin, 1975. 66, 67: Hirmer Fotoarchiv, Munich (3)—from *The Hittites and Their Contemporaries in Asia Minor* by J. G. Macqueen, Thames and Hudson, London, 1986. 68: Robert Frerck/Odyssey. 69: Slavonic Division, New York Public Library, Astor, Lenox and Tilden Foundations. 71: Robert Frerck /Woodfin Camp and Associates. 72: Peter Neve, Malente. 73: Museum of Anatolian Civilizations, Ankara; Hirmer Fotoarchiv, Munich—reconstruction by O. Puchstein from *Ancient Architecture* by S. Lloyd and H. W. Muller, Electra Editrice, Milan, 1972. 74: Richard Nowitz; Lotus Film/Eberhard Thiem, courtesy the Archaeological Museum, Ankara. 75: Robert Frerck/Odyssey—reconstruction by O. Puchstein from *Ḫattuša-Stadt der Götter und Tempel* by Peter Neve, Verlag Philipp von Zabern, Mainz, 1993. 76, 77: Mehmet Biber and Ajan Biber—reconstruction by W. Schirmer from *Der Alte Orient* by Winfried Orthmann, Propyläen Verlag, Berlin, 1975; Peter Neve, Malente. 78: Antalya Museum, Antalya. 80: The University Museum, The University of Pennsylvania. 81: James Whitmore/LIFE. 82: The University of Manchester, England. 83: Jean-Loup Charmet, Paris. 84, 85: The University Museum, The University of Pennsylvania. 86: Antalya Museum, Ankara. 87-89: Museum of Anatolian Civilizations, Ankara. 91: Peter Woolfitt/Robert Harding Picture Library, London—© The British Museum, London. 92: Prähistorische Staatssammlung, Munich—The Israel Museum, Jerusalem/Les Arcs, Ebnother Collection; Staatliche Museen zu Berlin-Preussischer Kulturbesitz, Vorderasiatisches Museum/photo by Jürgen Liepe. 93: The Metropolitan Museum of Art, gift of Nathaniel Spear Jr., 1977 (1977.186); Badisches Landesmuseum, Karlsruhe. 94: Bible Lands Museum Collection, Jerusalem. 95: Museum für Kunst und Gewerbe, Hamburg, Inv.Nr. 1962.40, photo: Museum (Maria Thrun). 97: Ozgen Acar/Sipa Press. 98, 99: Museum of Anatolian Civilizations, Ankara. 101: Photo Bulloz, Paris. 103: Gianni Dagli Orti, Paris—© The British Museum, London. 104, 105: Courtesy the Archaeological Exploration of Sardis. 107-117: Border art by John Drummond, Time-Life Books staff. 107: The Gordion Furniture Project. 108: The University Museum, The University of Pennsylvania—art by Elizabeth Simpson. 109: James Whitmore/ LIFE. 110: The University Museum, The University of Pennsylvania—Museum of Anatolian Civilizations, Ankara; art by Elizabeth Simpson. 111: Museum of Anatolian Civilizations, Ankara. 112: The University Museum, The University of Pennsylvania—The Gordion Furniture Project. 113: The Gordion Furniture Project—art by Elizabeth Simpson. 114: Lynn E. Roller, Associate Professor of Classics, The University of California at Davis. 115: The Gordion Furniture Project (2)—art by John Drummond, Time-Life Books staff, based on a drawing by Elizabeth Simpson. 116: The University Museum, The University of Pennsylvania—The Gordion Furniture Project. 117: The Bard Graduate Center for Studies in the Decorative Arts/The Museum of Anatolian Civilizations, Ankara—The Gordion Furniture Project; art by Elizabeth Simpson. 118: R.M.N., Paris. 122, 123: From *Classical Turkey* by John Freely, © Johnson Editions, Ltd., London, 1990; © The British Museum, London—Archiv für Kunst und Geschichte, Berlin. 127: Staatliche Museen zu Berlin-Preussischer Kulturbesitz, Antikensammlung—© Adam Woolfitt/Woodfin Camp and Associates. 128, 129: © The British Museum, London. 130, 131: Bodrum Museum, Bodrum. 133: CNES 1986-Distribution Spot Image/Université de Nantes, Laboratoire de Géographie Physique. 134: Hirmer Fotoarchiv, Munich—Institut für Klassische Archäologie, Universität Wien, Lykien Archiv/photo by W. Schiele. 135: Anadolu Ajansi, Ankara. 136: Machteld Mellink. 137: © The British Museum, London. 138: © Sheila Nardulli. 139: © The British Museum, London. 141: © Adam Woolfitt /Robert Harding Picture Library, London. 142, 143: Inset Emily Teeter; © Adam Woolfitt/Robert Harding Picture Library, London. 144, 145: Inset © Adam Woolfitt/Robert Harding Picture Library, London; Sunny Reynolds. 147: Staatliche Museen zu Berlin-Preussischer Kulturbesitz, Antikensammlung, photo by Jürgen Liepe. 149: Robert Lindley Vann. 150: © Adam Woolfitt/Woodfin Camp and Associates—German Archaeological Institute, Instanbul Division. 151: Robert Lindley Vann—German Archaeological Institute, Istanbul (3). 152: © Adam Woolfitt/Woodfin Camp and Associates—C. M. Dixon, Canterbury, Kent. 153: Robert Lindley Vann (2); R.M.N./Christian Larrieu, Paris. 154: Juliette de la Genière—Robert Lindley Vann. 155: Robert Lindley Vann—Dale Brown. 156: Professor Ekrem Akurgal, Izmir —Robert Lindley Vann. 157: Archiv für Kunst und Geschichte, Berlin/ courtesy Ephesus Archaeological Museum, Selcuk/photo by Erich Lessing. 158, 159: Art by Paul Breeden.

BIBLIOGRAPHY

BOOKS

Ainsworth, William Francis. *A Personal Narrative of the Euphrates Expedition.* Vol. 1. London: Kegan Paul, Trench, 1888.

Akşit, Ilhan. *Touristic Guide of Turkey.* Translated by Robert Bragner. Istanbul: Akşit Kültür Turizm Sanat Ajans, 1993.

Akurgal, Ekrem:
Ancient Civilizations and Ruins of Turkey. Istanbul: NET Turistik Yayınlar A.Ş., 1993.
The Art of the Hittites. Translated by Constance McNab. New York: Harry N. Abrams, 1962.

Alexander, Robert L. *The Sculpture and Sculptors of Yazilikaya.* Newark: University of Delaware Press, 1986.

Alkim, U. Bahadir. *Anatolia I: From the Beginnings to the End of the 2nd Millennium B.C.* Translated by James Hogarth. London: Barrie & Rockliff: The Cresset Press, 1969.

Amiet, Pierre. *Art of the Ancient Near East.* Translated by John Shepley and Claude Choquet. New York: Harry N. Abrams, 1977.

Bean, George E.:
Aegean Turkey. London: Ernest Benn, 1979.
Lycian Turkey: An Archaeological Guide. London: Ernest Benn, 1978.
Turkey beyond the Maeander: An Archaeological Guide. London: Ernest Benn, 1971.

Behr, Charles A. *Aelius Aristides and the Sacred Tales.* Amsterdam: Adolf M. Hakkert, 1968.

Bittel, Kurt:
Guide to Boğazköy. Ankara: 1972.
Hattusha: The Capital of the Hittites. New York: Oxford University Press, 1970.

Boardman, John. *The Greeks Overseas: Their Early Colonies and Trade.* London: Thames and Hudson, 1980.

Boardman, John, et al., eds. *The Cambridge Ancient History.* Vol. 3. Cambridge: Cambridge University Press, 1982.

Boyd, Mildred. *The Silent Cities: Civilizations Lost and Found.* New York: Criterion Books, 1966.

Brewster, Harry. *Classical Anatolia: The Glory of Hellenism.* London: I. B. Tauris, 1993.

Burenhult, Goran. *People of the Stone Age: Hunter-Gatherers and Early Farmers* (The Illustrated History of Humankind series). New York: HarperCollins, 1993.

Cavendish, Richard, ed. *Man, Myth & Magic: The Illustrated Encyclopedia of Mythology, Religion and the Unknown.* New York: Marshall Cavendish, 1983.

Ceram, C. W. *The Secret of the Hittites.* Translated by Richard and Clara Winston. New York: Alfred A. Knopf, 1956.

Ceram, C. W., ed. *Hands on the Past: Pioneer Archaeologists Tell Their Own Story.* New York: Alfred A. Knopf, 1966.

Cirlot, J. E. *A Dictionary of Symbols.* New York: Dorset Press, 1971.

Clayton, Peter A., and Martin J. Price. *The Seven Wonders of the Ancient World.* London: Routledge, 1989.

Collon, Dominique. *Near Eastern Seals: Interpreting the Past.* London: British Museum Publications, 1990.

Cook, Robert M. *Greek Painted Pottery.* London: Methuen, 1972.

De Vries, Keith, ed. *From Athens to Gordion: The Papers of a Memorial Symposium for Rodney S. Young.* Philadelphia: The University Museum, University of Pennsylvania, 1980.

Edwards, I. E. S., et al., eds. *The Cambridge Ancient History.* Vol.2, Parts 1 and 2. Cambridge: Cambridge University Press, 1975.

Egypt: Land of the Pharaohs (Lost Civilizations series). Alexandria, Va.: Time-Life Books, 1992.

Fellows, Charles. *An Account of Discoveries in Lycia, Being a Journal Kept During a Second Excursion in Asia Minor, 1840.* London: John Murray, 1841.

Frankfort, Henri. *The Art and Architecture of the Ancient Orient.* London: Penguin Books, 1989.

Freely, John. *The Western Shores of Turkey.* London: John Murray, 1988.

Ghirshman, Roman. *Iran: Parthians and Sassanians.* Translated by Stuart Gilbert and James Emmons. London: Thames and Hudson, 1962.

Gurney, O. R. *The Hittites.* London: Penguin Books, 1990.

Hamblin, Dora Jane, and the Editors of Time-Life Books. *The First Cities* (The Emergence of Man series). New York: Time-Life Books, 1973.

Hamilton, William J. *Researches in Asia Minor, Pontus, and Armenia; with Some Account of Their Antiquities and Geology.* Vol. 1. London: John Murray, 1842.

Haspels, C. H. Emilie. *The Highlands of Phrygia: Sites and Monuments.* Vol. 1. Princeton, N.J.: Princeton University Press, 1971.

Hicks, Jim, and the Editors of Time-Life Books. *The Empire Builders* (The Emergence of Man series). New York: Time-Life Books, 1974.

Hogarth, David G. *The Wandering Scholar.* London: Oxford University Press, 1925.

Knauth, Percy, and the Editors of Time-Life Books. *The Metalsmiths* (Emergence of Man series). New York: Time-Life Books, 1974.

Lloyd, Seton. *Ancient Turkey: A Traveller's History of Anatolia.* London: The British Museum Press, 1989.

The McGraw-Hill Encyclopedia of World Biography. New York: McGraw-Hill, 1973.

Macqueen, J. G. *The Hittites and Their Contemporaries in Asia Minor.* London: Thames and Hudson, 1986.

Mellaart, James. *The Archaeology of Ancient Turkey.* London: The Bodley Head, 1978.

The Metropolitan Museum of Art: Egypt and the Ancient Near East. New York: The Metropolitan Museum of Art, 1987.

Muscarella, Oscar White. *Bronze and Iron: Ancient Near Eastern Artifacts in the Metropolitan Museum of Art.* New York: The Metropolitan Museum of Art, 1988.

Muscarella, Oscar White, ed. *Ancient Art: The Norbert Schimmel Collection.* Mainz: Philipp von Zabern, 1974.

Neve, Peter. *Ḫattuša-Stadt der Götter und Tempel.* Mainz: Philipp von Zabern, 1993.

Orthmann, Winfried. *Der Alte Orient.* Berlin: Propyläen Verlag, 1975.

Parke, H. W. *The Oracles of Apollo in Asia Minor.* London: Croom Helm, n.d.

Pennick, Nigel. *The Ancient Science of Geomancy: Man in Harmony with the Earth.* London: Thames and Hudson, 1979.

Ramses II: Magnificence on the Nile (Lost Civilizations series). Alexandria, Va.: Time-Life Books, 1993.

Roaf, Michael. *Mesopotamia and the Ancient Near East* (Cultural Atlas of the World series). Alexandria, Va.: Stonehenge Press, 1990.

Slatter, Enid. *Xanthus: Travels of Discovery in Turkey.* London: Rubicon Press, 1994.

Smith, Whitney. *Flags: Through the Ages and across the World.* San Francisco: McGraw-Hill , 1975.

Sobel, Christa. *Ephesus.* Istanbul: Hitit Color, 1990.

Soden, Wolfram von. *The Ancient Orient.* Translated by Donald G. Schley. Grand Rapids: William B. Eerdmans, 1994.

Splendors of the Past (Lost Cities of the Ancient World series). Washington, D.C.: National Geographic Society, 1981.

Stillwell, Richard, ed. *The Princeton Encyclopedia of Classical Sites.* Princeton, N.J.: Princeton University Press, 1976.

Stoneman, Richard. *A Traveller's History of Turkey.* New York: Interlink Books, 1993.

Summers, G. D. *Tille Höyük 4: The Late Bronze Age and the Iron Age Transition.* Ankara: The British Institute of Archaeology, 1993.

Tadmor, H., and M. Weinfeld, eds. *History, Historiography and Interpretation: Studies in Biblical and Cuneiform Literatures.* Jerusalem: Magnes Press, 1983.

Todd, Ian A. *Çatal Hüyük in Perspective.* Menlo Park, Calif.: Cummings Publishing, 1976.

Tuchelt, Klaus. *Branchidai-Didyma.* Mainz: Philipp von Zabern, 1992.

Vandenberg, Philipp. *The Mystery of the Oracles.* New York: Macmillan, 1982.

Wartke, Ralf-Bernhard. *Urartu das Reich am Ararat.* Mainz: Philipp von Zabern, 1993.

Wood, J. T. *Discoveries at Ephesus.* London: Longmans, Green, 1877.

Yalman, Ahmed Emin. *Turkey in My Time.* Norman: University of Oklahoma Press, 1956.

Young, Rodney S. *Three Great Early Tumuli: The Gordion Excavations Final Reports.* Vol. 1. Philadelphia: The University Museum, University of Pennsylvania, 1981.

PERIODICALS

Acar, Özgen. "Karun Hazinesi." *Thy Sky,* November 1993.

American Journal of Archaeology, Vol. 96, No. 1, January 1992.

American Journal of Archaeology, Vol. 99, No. 2, 1995.

Bammer, Anton. "Recent Excavations at the Altar of Artemia in Ephesus." *Archaeology,* July 1974.

Biblical Archaeologist, June/September 1989.

Bittel, Kurt. "The Great Temple of Hattusha-Boğazköy." *American Journal of Archaeology,* Winter 1976.

Braidwood, Robert J. "The Origin and Growth of a Research Focus: Agricultural Beginnings." *Expedition* (University of Pennsylvania), Vol. 28, No. 2, 1986.

Brown, Dale "Romancing the Stones." *Los Angeles Times,* February 5, 1995.

Canby, Jeanny Vorys:
"The Sculptors of the Hittite Capital." *Oriens Antiqvvs,* Vol. 15, 1976.
"The Walters Gallery Cappadocian Tablet and the Sphinx in Anatolia in the Second Millennium B.C." *Journal of Near Eastern Studies* (University of Chicago), October 1975.

Collins, Billie Jean, ed. "Newsletter for Anatolian Studies," Vol. 10, 1994.

De Vries, Keith. "Gordion and Phrygia in the Sixth Century B.C." *Source: Notes in the History of Art,* Spring/Summer 1988.

Esin, Ufuk, et al. "Salvage Excavations at the Pre-Pottery Site of Aşikli Höyük in Central Anatolia." *Anatolica,* Vol. 17, 1991.

Gates, Marie-Henriette. "Archaeology in Turkey." *American Journal of Archaeology,* January 1994.

Goell, Theresa. "Throne above the Euphrates." *National Geographic,* March 1961.

Greenewalt, Crawford H., Jr. "When a Mighty Empire Was Destroyed: The Common Man at the Fall of Sardis, ca. 546 B.C." *Proceedings of the American Philosophical Society* (University of California at Berkeley), Vol. 136, No. 2, 1992.

Haselberger, Lothar. "The Construction Plans for the Temple of Apollo at Didyma." *Scientific American,* December 1985.

Kosay, Hamit Zubeyr. "A Great Discovery." *Illustrated London News,* July 21, 1945.

Mellaart, James. "A Neolithic City in Turkey." *Scientific American,* April 1964.

Mellink, Machteld J.:
"Archaeology in Turkey." *American Journal of Archaeology,* January 1991.
"Archaeology in Turkey." *American Journal of Archaeology,* January 1992.
"The City of Midas." *Scientific American,* July 1959.
"Excavations at Karataş-Semayük and Elmali, Lycia, 1970." *American Journal of Archaeology,* July 1971.

Özgüç, Tahsin. "An Assyrian Trading Outpost." *Scientific American,* February 1963.

Prag, A. J. N. W. "Reconstructing King Midas: A First Report." *Anatolian Studies: Journal of the British Institute of Archaeology at Ankara,* Vol. 39, 1989.

Roller, Lynn E.:
"The Great Mother at Gordion: The Hellenization of an Anatolian Cult." *Journal of Hellenic Studies,* 1991.
"The Legend of Midas." *Classical Antiquity,* University of California Press, October 1983.
"Phrygian Myth and Cult." *Source: Notes in the History of Art,* Spring/Summer 1988.

Sams, G. Kenneth. "Beer in the City of Midas." *Archaeology,* March 1977.

Simpson, Elizabeth:
"'Midas' Bed' and a Royal Phrygian Funeral." *Journal of Field Archaeology,* Vol. 17, 1990.
"The Phrygian Artistic Intellect." *Source: Notes in the History of Art,* Spring/Summer 1988.
"Reconstructing an Ancient Table." *Expedition* (University of Pennsylvania), Summer 1983.

Simpson, Elizabeth, and Robert Payton. "Royal Wooden Furniture from Gordion." *Archaeology,* November/December 1986.

Ward, Diane Raines. "In Turkey, a Race to Rescue the Past." *Smithsonian,* August 1990.

Whitmore, James. "A Mighty King's Paneled Tomb." *Life,* August 5, 1957.

OTHER SOURCES

"The Anatolian Civilizations Museum." Guidebook. Ankara, n.d.

"Antalya Museum." Catalog. Ankara, November 1992.

Åström, Paul, ed. "High, Middle or Low?" Paper presented at an International Colloquium on Absolute Chronology held at the University of Gothenburg, August 1987.

"Bible Lands Museum Jerusalem." Guidebook. Jerusalem, 1992.

"Carian Princess." Brochure. Ankara: Bodrum Museum of Underwater Archaeology, 1993.

"Ephesus Museum Catalogue." Istanbul: Ephesus Museum, 1989.

Hodder, Ian. "Contextual Archaeology: An Interpretation of Catal Hüyük and a Discussion of the Origins of Agriculture." *Institute of Archaeology Golden Jubilee Bulletin*. London: University of London Institute of Archaeology, 1987.

"The Lydian Hoard." Brochure. Ankara: Anatolian Civilizations Museum, November 19, 1993.

Neve, Peter. "Hattusha-Boğazköy." In *The Archaeology of Anatolia: An Encyclopedia*. Ed. by G. K. Sams, 1992.

"Woman in Anatolia: 9000 Years of the Anatolian Woman." Catalog. Istanbul: Topkapi Sarayi Museum, 1993.

INDEX

Bin Tepe: excavation of Lydian tombs at, 103-104
Bittel, Kurt: 67; excavations by, 44, 53, 54, 58-59, 71
Black Sea: 10, 129; Greek colonies on, 120, 133
Bodrum: 130, 136. *See also* Halicarnassus
Boeotia: 124
Boghazkäle: 7, 42. *See also* Boghazköy
Boghazköy (Boghazkäle): 7, 8, 13, 43-44, 47, 69; cuneiform tablets found at, 18, 42, 45-46, 48, 54, 56, 64, 71; excavations at, 45-46, 47, 53, 56
Bosporus: 53, 120, 133
Bossert, Helmuth T.: 48
Braidwood, Robert J.: 34
Branchidae: 152
British Institute of Archaeology: 15
British Museum: 21, 136, 137, 146
British School (Athens): 129
Brutus: 146
Burckhardt, Johann Ludwig: 39
Byzantine Empire: 13, 22, 159
Byzantium: 159
Büyükkale: 46, 53

C

Caesar, Julius: 11
Caicus River: 121, 138
Cambel, Halet: 34
Candaules: 96, 100
Capture of Miletus, The: 134
Carchemish: 42, 51, 62-63; reliefs found near, *50*
Carians: 120, 121, 124, 126, 128, 134, 135, 138
Caucasus Mountains: 53, 159
Caunus: tombs at, *138*
Cayster River: 14, 121
Chantre, Ernest: 45
Chatal Höyük: 29; excavations at, 26-28, *36;* statues found at, *23, 29, 37, 158;* wall relief found at, *37*
Chayönü: 158; artifacts found at, *35;* excavations at, *34, 35*
Chimera Tomb: *17*
Church of Saint John: 136, *156*
Cimmerians: 12, 85, 88, 95, 100, 103, 136, 159
Claros: temple at, *154, 155*
Claudius: 147
Cleopatra: 139
Cnidos: 128
Codrus: 125
Colophon: 100, 122, 132

Commagene: 141, 147-148
Constantine: 159
Constantinople: 13, 159
Corinth: 101
Cornell University: 96, 101, 103
Cos: 128
Crete: 122, 124, 126
Crimea: 88
Croesus: 8, 12, 85, 86, 96, *101,* 102, 103, 104-105, 121, 136, 140
Curtius, Ludwig: 46
Cyme: 124
Cyprus: 140
Cyrus the Great: 8, 12, 100, 105, 106, 121, 159

D

Darius I: 12, 87, 134
Darius III: 12
Delphi: shrine at, 86, 100, 102, 105, 107, 132, 149, 152
DeVries, Keith: 86
Diana (deity): 156. *See also* Artemis
Didyma: temple at, *149, 152, 153*
Dionysus (deity): 86
Dorians: 120, 126, 128, 140

E

Eastern Roman Empire: *See* Byzantine Empire
East Greeks: 120; daily life, 129; trade, 128-129, 159
Egypt: 11, 12, 44, 45, 63, 69, 126, 139, 140, 147, 158; treaty with Hittites, 64-68
Egyptians: 39, 41, 42, 90
Elgin Marbles: 146
Empire of the Hittites, The: 42
Ephesus: 122, 125, 136, 137, 156, 159; excavations at, 14-17, *18-19*
Erlach, Johann Fischer von: drawing by, *122-123*
Esin, Ufuk: 32
Eskisehir: 86
Etruria: 100, 129
Eumenes: 138
Euphrates River: 15, 29, 42, 44, 55, 62, 148, 159

F

Fellows, Sir Charles: 7, *16,* 137, 146; explorations by, 13-14

G

Galatians: 138
German Archaeological Institute: 71
Germanicus Caesar: 154
German Oriental Society: 71
Goell, Theresa: excavations at Nemrud Dagh, 147-148
Golden Fleece: 120
Göltepe: smelting of tin at, 22-25
Gordion: 12, 85, 87, 95, 100, 103, 104; excavations at, 79, *80, 81,* 82-83, *85,* 86, 87-89, *107-117*
Gordion Furniture Project: 107
Gordion knot: 85-86
Gordius: 85
Granicus River: 12
Grave goods: 21, *24, 81,* 82-84, *88, 89, 130-131*
Graverobbers: 97, 104
Great Altar of Zeus: 139
Great Temple (Hattusha): *See* Hattusha
Great Temple of Diana: *See* Temple of Diana
Greece: 96, 121, 122, 126; trade with, 91, 102
Greeks: 10, 20, 84, 85, 86, 88, 106; colonization of coastal Anatolia, 12, 84, 96, 100, 102, 105, 119-122, 124-129, 159
Green, W. Kirby: 39, 40
Greenewalt, Crawford H., Jr.: 105
Gygean Lake: 103
Gyges: 96, 100, 101, 102, 103, 104, 106

H

Hacilar: 158; excavations at, 26, 27
Hadrian: 159
Hadrian's Temple (Ephesus): *159*
Halicarnassus (Bodrum): 12, 127, 128, 134; tomb and grave goods found at, *130-131. See also* Mausoleum of Halicarnassus
Halys River: 87, 103, 105
Hama (Hamath): inscribed stones at, 39-40, 41, 42
Hamath: *See* Hama
Hamilton, Sir William: 10, 11, 20, 49; sketches by, *9*
Hammurabi: 44
Hantawiya: 56
Hantili: 55
Hanzusra: 56
Haruwanduli: 56
Harvard University: 96, 101, 103
Hashshu: 54
Hatti: 42, 55, 62, 63, 68, 69

Sicilians: 70

Simpson, Elizabeth: 107, 108, 114, 117; conservation of Phrygian woodworking, *112, 116. See also* Gordion Furniture Project

Smenkhkare: 63

Smyrna (Izmir): 14, 100, 103, 129; relocation of, 132. *See also* Bayrakli

Sobek (deity): bronze, *154*

Society for Biblical Archaeology: 42

Solomon: 41, 42

Solon: 106

Sphinx Gate (Hattusha): 60, 72, 73, 74; bronze tablet found at, *59;* sculpture from, *40*

Spirydowicz, Krysia: 107

Strabo: 125, 132, 136

Subhi Pasha: 40

Sumer: 22, 29, 86

Susa: 134

Syria: 55, 69

Syrians: 41, 42

T

Tabal: 84

Tacitus: 154

Tarhuntassa: 58

Tarsus: 159

Tartessus: 129

Taurus Mountains: 10, 12, 22, 26, 48, 54, 158

Tavium: 7

Telipinu: 55, 56, 62

Tell el-Amarna: cuneiform tablets found at, 45, 47

Temple of Apollo (Claros): *154, 155*

Temple of Apollo (Didyma), *149, 152, 153*

Temple of Artemis: *See* Temple of Diana

Temple of Diana (Ephesus): 14, 17, 20, 120, *122-123, 156;* gold plaques found at, *21. See also* Artemision

Teshub (deity): relief of, *49*

Texier, Charles: 9, 13, 18, 42, 49, 71; explorations by, 7-8

Textiles: early examples of, 28, *35*

Tezcan, Burhan: *81*

Thales: 133-134

Thebes: 47

Thessaly: 124

Tiberius: 154

Tigris River: 15, 29

Tille Höyük: *15*

Tiwatapara: 56-57

Tmolus Mountains: 96

Trade: Anatolian routes, 62, 87, 96, 148; Assyrian, 19, 56-57; and East Greeks, 128-129, 159; Egyptian grain, 147; evidence of at Chatal Höyük, 28; Lydia, 101; Pergamon, 138; Urartu, 91

Treaty of Kadesh: 45; tablet inscribed with, *68*

Trojans: 126, 132, 140

Troy: 18, 84, 124, 158

Tudhaliya IV: 44, 45, 53, 58, 65; relief of, *67, 68*

Turkey: encouragement of archaeological projects by, 11, 18-19

Turkish Antiquities Service: 81

Turkish Department of Antiquities: 15

Tushpa: *91*

Tutankhamen: 63, 107

U

Ugarit: 69

University of Ankara: 83, 94, 129

University of Chicago: 22, 34

University of Istanbul: 48

University of Pennsylvania: 80, 88, 107

Urartu: 12, 83, 91

Uygur, Nazif: *116*

V

Virgin Mary: 138, 156

W

Weather god (deity): 39, 60, 61, 63; re-

lief of, *67*

Winckler, Hugo: 62, 71; excavations at Boghazköy, 45-46, 47, 64

Wood, John Turtle: excavations at Ephesus, 14-17, *18-19*

Woodworking: Phrygian, 83, *107, 108, 112, 113, 115, 116, 117*

Wright, William: 39-40, 41, 42, 43, 52

Writing: Assyrian cuneiform tablets found at Kanesh, 19; decipherment of Hittite inscriptions, 11-12, 40-42, 45-48, 52, 55; Hamathite inscriptions, 39-42, 48; parchment, 139

X

Xanthus: 140; excavations at, 146; sarcophagus found at, *139*

Xanthus River: *133,* 140

Xerxes: 121

Y

Yarimburgaz: excavation of caves at, 28

Yassihöyük: 79; carved relief found at, *84;* excavations at, 87-88

Yazilikaya: carvings at, 7-8, *9,* 42, *65-67;* temple at, *65,* 68

Yenner, Aslihan: excavations at Göltepe, 22-24

Young, Rodney S.: 87, 112, 116; excavations at Gordion, 80, *81,* 82-83, 86, 87-90, 94, 107, 108; excavations at Kücük Höyük, 95, 96

Z

Zeus (deity): altar to, 139

Zeus-Ahura Mazda (deity): 141, 147; statue of, *144-145*

Zeus Basileus (deity): 85

Zonguldak: 81

BLACK SEA

BOSPORUS

Byzantium

GORDION SITULA

HITTITE WAR GOD

Alaca Höyük

Hattusha • Yazilikaya

Ankara

Gordion

Kane

Troy

Sangarius River

CENTRAL
ANATOLIAN
PLATEAU

Ashikli Höyük

LESBOS

Mytilene

Pergamon

Sardis

Hermus River

Smyrna

Cayster River

CHIOS

Claros

Ephesus

Maeander River

Miletus

SAMOS

Priene

Didyma

Halicarnassus

LYCIAN TOMB

Chatal Höyük

TAURUS MOUNTAINS

Tarsus

Mersin

Antalya

AEGEAN SEA

COS

Cnidos

Xanthus

Patara

RHODES

NEOLITHIC IDOL

CYPRUS

MEDITERRANEAN SEA

CRETE